THREE OF A KIND
QUIZZES

D0353783

First published in 2002 by Miles Kelly Publishing Ltd,
Bardfield Centre, Great Bardfield, Essex, CM7 4SL

Copyright © Miles Kelly Publishing Ltd 2002

This edition printed 2002

ISBN 1-84236-135-X

2 4 6 8 10 9 7 5 3

Project Manager: Ian Paulyn
Assistant: Lisa Clayden
Design: Clare Sleven

Contact us by email: info@mileskelly.net
Website: www.mileskelly.net

Printed in India

THREE OF A KIND QUIZZES

by
Christopher Rigby

Miles Kelly
PUBLISHING

About the Author

Born in Blackburn, Lancashire in 1960, Christopher Rigby has been compiling and presenting pub quizzes for the past 15 years. When he is not adding to his material for quizzes, Christopher works in the car industry. He is married to Clare – they have two teenage daughters, Hollie and Ashley and share their home with two demented dogs called Vespa and Bailey. A keen Manchester United fan Christopher lists his heroes as George Best and Homer Simpson.

THREE OF A KIND EXPLAINED

This quiz book comprises 900 questions each of which requires three answers. Below are two examples:

1. Which are the three closest planets to the sun? (Mercury, Venus and Earth)
2. What name is given to a young? A. Cow B. Cat C. Goat (A. Calf B. Kitten C. Kid)

QUIZ ONE

1. Which three English resorts are collectively known as Torbay?
2. Which three internal organs are involved in a triple transplant?
3. John Higgins became the 4th John to win the World Snooker Championship. Name the previous three.
4. Name the backing groups of the following singers. A. Dion B. Lloyd Cole C. Rocky Sharpe
5. Into which three categories are Shakespeare plays placed?
6. King Canute ruled which three countries?
7. Which three male Robinsons have presented the BBC's *Points of View*?
8. What do the following scientific instruments measure? A. Craniometer B. Lactometer C. Hygrometer
9. What were the names of the three Popes of 1978?
10. What are the most common surnames in the following countries? A. Germany B. China C. Sweden

ANSWERS

1. Torquay, Paignton & Brixham 2. Heart, liver & lungs 3. John Parrott, John Spencer & John Pulman 4. A. Belmonts B. Commotions C. Replays 5. Tragedies, comedies & histories. 6. England, Denmark & Norway 7. Robert, Kenneth & Tony 8. A. Skull size B. Milk density C. Humidity 9. John Paul I, John Paul II & Paul VI 10. A. Schultz B. Chang C. Johannsen

QUIZ TWO

1. Who with the surname of Williams had No. 1 hits with
   A. 'She's The One' B. 'Moon River' C. 'Free'?

2. In 1989 four European Communist countries lost power. One
   was Czechoslovakia, name the other three.

3. What names are given to the three main parts of a comet?

4. Whose life stories are chronicled in the following
   autobiographies? A. *The Naked Civil Servant* B. *Where's the Rest
   of Me* C. *Spend, Spend, Spend*

5. Name the film stars who died whilst making the following films.
   A. *Game of Death* in 1973 B. *The Return of the Musketeers* in
   1989 C. *Brainstorm* in 1981

6. Who were the last three Poet Laureates of the 20th century?

7. What are the titles of the first three UK No. 1 hit singles of the
   Spice Girls?

8. What are the only three female first names that feature in the
   titles of Shakespeare plays?

9. In which fictional towns are the following TV programmes set?
   A. *Postman Pat* B. *Home and Away* C. *All Creatures Great
   and Small*

10. What is the main river of A. Rome B. Washington
    C. Amsterdam?

QUIZ THREE

1. The Drifters, Elton John and David Bowie all had a hit record with the word 'Saturday' in the title. Name the three songs.

2. Name the three films from the following publicity blurbs. A. We are not alone B. An adventure 65 million years in the making C. When the hands point straight up the excitement starts.

3. What are the three highest mountains in the world?

4. What are the three largest planets in the solar system?

5. What are the three fire signs of the zodiac?

6. Who were the first three wives of Henry VIII?

7. In *Dad's Army* what were the day-time jobs of A. Captain Mainwaring B. Corporal Jones C. Private Frasier?

8. Excluding England, in which three countries do tennis Grand Slam Tournaments take place?

9. Which three Scottish football clubs have a compass point in their names?

10. Name the three American states that have five letters in their name.

ANSWERS

1. The Drifters sang 'Saturday Night at the Movies', Elton sang 'Saturday Night's Alright for Fighting' & Bowie sang 'Drive In Saturday'. 2. A. *Close Encounters of the Third Kind* B. *Jurassic Park* C. *High Noon* 3. Everest, K2 & Kangchenjunga 4. Jupiter, Saturn & Uranus 5. Leo, Aries & Sagittarius 6. Catherine of Aragon, Anne Boleyn & Jane Seymour 7. A. Bank Manager B. Butcher C. Undertaker 8. France, Australia & the USA 9. East Fife, East Stirling & Queen of the South 10. Texas, Idaho & Maine

QUIZ FOUR

1. Which were the first three football clubs beginning with the letter C to win the FA Cup?

2. Pete, Stuart and Tony were all one-time members of the Beatles. What were their surnames?

3. At the 2000 Sydney Olympics how many gold, silver and bronze medals were won by the UK?

4. Traditionally a string quartet consists of which three different instruments?

5. Which three European countries joined the EU in 1995?

6. How many cents are there in a A. Dime B. Dollar C. Nickel?

7. Which three racecourses host the classics in the English flat season?

8. What are the chemical symbols of A. Gold B. Lead C. Tin?

9. In the American sitcom *Roseanne* what are the names of her three oldest children?

10. What are the animal nicknames of A. Derby County FC B. Millwall FC C. Leicester City FC?

QUIZ FIVE

1. What are the first names of the Andrews Sisters?

2. Name the famous mothers of A. Shirley Williams B. Edward VI
   C. Mia Farrow.

3. Name the brotherly pop groups who had hits with A. 'Bye Bye
   Love' B. 'The Sun Ain't Gonna Shine Anymore'
   C. 'Let Your Love Flow'.

4. Name the famous sisters of A. Lorna Luft B. Loretta Lynn
   C. Warren Beatty.

5. What are the surnames of the family members in the following
   pop groups? A. Oasis B. The Beach Boys C. Five Star

6. What are the names of the central families in the following
   sitcoms? A. *Butterflies* B. *Happy Days* C. *The Cosby Show*

7. Name the famous fathers of A. Mrs Norman Cook B. Cherie
   Blair C. Carrie Fisher.

8. In which years were the following born? A. Prince Charles
   B. Prince Edward C. Prince Andrew

9. On TV who played A. JR Ewing B. Bobby Ewing C. Gary Ewing?

10. Name the brothers that appeared together in the following films.
    A. *Young Guns* B. *The Fabulous Baker Boys* C. *Kojak: The
    Belarus File*

QUIZ SIX

1. Name the three musical instruments beginning with the letter T that feature in the brass section of an orchestra.

2. In the sitcom *It Ain't Half Hot Mum* who played A. Lofty B. Gloria C. Sergeant Major Williams?

3. People suffering from the following phobias have a morbid fear of what? A. Claustrophobia B. Brontophobia C. Blennophobia

4. In which American states are the following? A. The Everglades B. The Hoover Dam C. Fort Knox

5. Who were the first three Manchester United players to be sent off whilst playing for United at Wembley?

6. Name the actors who played Richard Hannay in *The 39 Steps* in the following years A. 1935 B. 1959 C. 1978.

7. There are six gases which are collectively known as noble gases. Krypton, xenon and radon are three of them. Name the other three.

8. In January 2001 Scotland won the World Snooker Team Championships. Which trio of players made up the Scottish team?

9. Name the first three UK top 10 hit singles for the Australian entertainer Rolf Harris.

10. Four counties in the Republic of Ireland begin with the letter C. One is Carlow, name the other three.

ANSWERS

1. Trumpet, trombone & tuba 2. A. Don Estelle B. Melvyn Hayes C. Windsor Davies 3. A. Enclosed spaces B. Thunder C. Slime 4. A. Florida B. Colorado C. Kentucky 5. Kevin Moran, Andre Kanchelsis & Roy Keane 6. A. Robert Donat B. Kenneth More C. Robert Powell 7. Argon, neon & helium 8. Stephen Hendry, John Higgins & Alan McManus 9. 'Tie me Kangaroo Down Sport', 'Sun Arise' & 'Two Little Boys' 10. Cork, Clare & Cavan

QUIZ SEVEN

1. In the TV series *The Avengers* name the actresses who played
   A. Emma Peel B. Cathy Gale C. Tara King.
2. Name the first three footballers to win 100 caps for England.
3. Name the first three artists to win the Eurovision Song Contest for the UK.
4. Name the first three men to present the TV show *Stars In Their Eyes*.
5. Name the three famous horror movie actors who were all coincidentally born on May 27th.
6. In a TV sitcom what are the names of the three priests that share a house on Craggy Island?
7. The human brain consists of four lobes, one of which is called the occipital lobe. Name the other three.
8. The athlete Sebastian Coe once held three simultaneous world records over which three distances?
9. What are the names of the three longest bridges in the UK?
10. Who were the first three members of Take That to enjoy solo hits?

QUIZ EIGHT

....

1. In the children's TV programme *Play School* what shapes are the three windows?
2. Name the three English public schools that lend their name to versions of the game of fives.
3. What is the largest lake in A. England B. Scotland C. Ireland?
4. Which three planets are farthest away from the sun?
5. In *Coronation Street* who plays Jack, Vera and Terry Duckworth?
6. In the film *The Wizard of Oz* which characters were looking for A. Courage B. A heart C. A brain?
7. Name the capital cities of the following countries, all of which begin with the same letter. A. Iran B. Estonia C. Libya
8. What are the first names of the Bee Gees?
9. Excluding Tinky Winky what are the names of the Teletubbies?
10. In the Sherlock Holmes novels what were the names of his A. Brother B. Arch enemy C. Housekeeper?

QUIZ NINE

1. What gifts are traditionally given on the following wedding anniversaries? A. 10th B. 20th C. 30th

2. According to the nursery rhyme little boys are made of slugs and snails and puppy dog's tails. What are little girls made of?

3. What are the names of Tony Blair's three sons?

4. In 1984, 1985 and 1986 Everton reached the FA Cup Final. Name the three teams that opposed them in each final.

5. Which three gifts did the three wise men bring to the baby Jesus?

6. Alphabetically what are the last three star signs?

7. In which three American cities were the following TV programmes set? A. *Frasier* B. *Lou Grant* C. *The Golden Girls*

8. What are the titles of the first three films in which Clint Eastwood played Inspector Harry Callaghan?

9. Who along with Davy Jones made up the Monkees?

10. What do the initials stand for in the name of the author J R R Tolkien?

ANSWERS

1. A. Tin B. China C. Pearl 2. Sugar & spice & all things nice 3. Euan, Nicholas & Leo 4. 1984 – Watford, 1985 – Manchester United, 1986 – Liverpool 5. Gold, frankincense & myrrh 6. Scorpio, Taurus & Virgo 7. A. Seattle B. Los Angeles C. Miami 8. *Dirty Harry*, *Magnum Force* & *The Enforcer* 9. Micky Dolenz, Peter Tork & Mike Nesmith re10. John Ronald Reuel

QUIZ TEN

1. Name the three actresses who played the Witches of Eastwick.
2. What are the first names of The Three Stooges?
3. What are the titles of the first three James Bond films?
4. In the musical *Oliver* who played A. Fagin B. Bill Sykes
   C. Oliver Twist?
5. Who played Batman in the following films? A. *Batman Forever*
   B. *Batman Returns* C. *Batman and Robin*
6. Name the actors who played The Three Amigos.
7. Who played the title roles in the following *Carry On* films?
   A. *Carry On Henry* B. *Carry On Columbus* C. *Carry On Cleo*
8. In the film *Jaws* what were the surnames of the three
   characters who hunted the great white shark aboard a boat
   called the Orca?
9. In the film *Shirley Valentine* who played A. The title role
   B. Shirley's Greek lover C. Shirley's husband?
10. In the 2000 film version of *Charlie's Angels* name the three
    actresses who played the angels.

QUIZ ONE

1. What are the three scientific categories for which Nobel Prizes are awarded?

2. Who were the first three actors to play *Dr Who* on TV?

3. In which three years of the 20th century were Olympic Games cancelled due to war?

4. At which three lanes do the following football clubs play their home matches? A. Tottenham Hotspur B. Bury
C. Sheffield United

5. In the TV series *Red Dwarf* who played A. Rimmer B. Lister
C. Cat?

6. Name the three ballets composed by Tchaikovsky.

7. Who played Robin Hood in the following films? A. *Robin Hood, Prince of Thieves* B. *Robin & Marian* C. *Time Bandits*

8. In the Beatles song 'When I'm 64' what are the names of the three grandchildren?

9. What are the national flowers of A. India B. Australia C. Japan?

10. Name the three male members of the *Not The Nine O'Clock News* team.

QUIZ TWO

1. Excluding Devon, name the English counties that begin with the letter D.

2. How many yards are there in the following? A. Mile B. Chain C. Furlong

3. Name the three UK No. I hit singles of the 1980s that contain the word 'Red' in the title of the song.

4. Which three men appeared in *The Goons* with Peter Sellers?

5. For which three countries did the legendary Alfredo Di Stefano play international football?

6. What are the first names of the three female members of the 'popstars' group Hear'say?

7. In which films did Dustin Hoffman play the following characters? A. Benjamin Braddock B. Michael Dorsey C. Ratso Rizzo

8. Who are the arch-enemies of A. Flash Gordon B. Superman C. He Man?

9. In which year did the following TV programmes begin? A. *Coronation Street* B. *Top of the Pops* C. *EastEnders*

10. What are the three largest lakes in the world?

QUIZ THREE

1. Name the three horses that won the last three Grand Nationals of the 1990s.

2. In Roman numerals which three letters represent A. 50 B. 500 C. 1000?

3. What are the three names given to a male deer each of which contains four letters?

4. What are the world's three largest oceans?

5. Who sang the theme tunes for the following TV programmes?
   A. *Rawhide* B. *Brush Strokes* C. *One Foot In The Grave*

6. What are the three oldest clubs in the football league?

7. Which pop stars starred in the following films? A. *Ned Kelly*
   B. *The Man Who Fell To Earth* C. *Buster*

8. Which cities do the following American football teams come from? A. Dolphins B. Cowboys C. Bronchos

9. Name the three countries that have the largest Jewish population.

10. In 1979 who became the first three British footballers to be transferred for a fee of £1 million or more?

ANSWERS

1. 1997- Lord Gyllene, 1998 - Earth Summit, 1999 - Bobbyjo 2. A = L B = D C = M
3. Buck, stag & hart 4. Pacific, Atlantic & Indian 5. A. Frankie Laine B. Kevin Rowlands
C. Eric Idle 6. Notts County, Stoke City & Notts Forest 7. A. Mick Jagger B. David
Bowie C. Phil Collins 8. A. Miami B. Dallas C. Denver 9. USA, Israel & Russia
10. Trevor Francis, Steve Daley & Andy Gray

QUIZ FOUR

1. What are the three most filmed Shakespeare plays?
2. Who painted the following paintings? A. *The Haywain* B. *The Blue Boy* C. *Campbells' Soup Tins*
3. Name the three cities in which the first three public libraries in the UK were established.
4. What are the three largest deserts in the world?
5. Who played the President of the USA in the following films? A. *Dave* B. *Failsafe* C. *Airforce One*
6. What are the first names of the pop trio the Thompson Twins?
7. What three items are needed to perform an excommunication?
8. What are the capital cities of the following countries, all of which begin with the letter S? A. Bulgaria B. South Korea C. Sweden
9. Which literary characters went to sea in the following? A. Beautiful pea green boat B. Sieve C. With silver buckles on his knee
10. What were the first three full-length animated Disney films?

ANSWERS

1. *Hamlet, Romeo and Juliet and Macbeth* 2. A. John Constable B. Thomas Gainsborough C. Andy Warhol 3. Manchester, Liverpool & Sheffield 4. Sahara, Australian & Arabian 5. A. Kevin Kline B. Henry Fonda C. Harrison Ford 6. Joe, Tom & Alannah 7. Bell, book & candle 8. A. Sofia B. Seoul C. Stockholm 9. A. The Owl and the Pussycat B. The Jumblies C. Bobby Shaftoe 10. *Snow White & the Seven Dwarves, Pinocchio & Fantasia*

QUIZ FIVE

THE FOLLOWING TEN RECORDING ARTISTS ALL HAD THREE UK No 1 HITS IN THE 20TH CENTURY. NAME THE THREE SONGS IN EACH CASE.

1. Frank Sinatra

2. The Kinks

3. Wet, Wet, Wet

4. U2

5. Manfred Mann

6. Brotherhood Of Man

7. Roy Orbison

8. Adam and the Ants

9. Mud

10. Donny Osmond

ANSWERS

1. 'Three Coins In A Fountain', 'Strangers In The Night' & 'Somethin' Stupid'. 2. 'Sunny Afternoon', 'You Really Got Me' & 'Tired Of Waiting For You'. 3. 'With A Little Help From My Friends', 'Goodnight Girl' & 'Love Is All Around'. 4. 'Desire', 'The Fly' & 'Discotheque' 5. 'Do Wah Diddy Diddy', 'Pretty Flamingo' & 'Mighty Quinn'. 6. 'Save All Your Kisses For Me', 'Figaro' & 'Angelo'. 7. 'Only The Lonely', 'It's Over' & 'Oh Pretty Woman'. 8. 'Stand & Deliver', 'Prince Charming' & 'Goody Two Shoes'. 9. 'Tiger Feet', 'Oh Boy' & 'Lonely This Christmas'. 10. 'Puppy Love', 'The Twelfth Of Never' & 'Young Love'.

QUIZ SIX

1. Which three James Bond themes were performed by Shirley Bassey?

2. Which three actresses were nominated for nine Oscars or more in the 20th century?

3. Name the three countries beginning with the letter M that border China.

4. At what grounds do England, Scotland and Ireland play their home Rugby Union matches?

5. What is the name of King Arthur's A. Magician B. Sword C. Shield?

6. Name the three people who played the New Avengers.

7. Which were the first three countries to build a Disney theme park?

8. The Equator passes through which three South American countries?

9. In the sitcom *Only Fools and Horses* who played A. Cassandra B. Trigger C. Uncle Albert?

10. What three words represent the initials of the internet company AOL ?

ANSWERS

1. *Goldfinger, Diamonds Are Forever & Moonraker* 2. Katherine Hepburn, Bette Davis & Meryl Streep 3. Mongolia, Macau & Myanmar 4. Twickenham, Murrayfield & Landsowne Road 5. A. Merlin B. Excalibur C. Pridwen 6. Patrick Macnee, Gareth Hunt & Joanna Lumley 7. USA, France & Japan 8. Ecuador, Brazil & Colombia 9. A. Gwyneth Strong B. Roger Lloyd Pack C. Buster Merryfield 10. America On Line

QUIZ SEVEN

1. Name the three men who hosted *Juke Box Jury* in the 20th century.

2. Which recording artists had hits with the following 'Black' songs?
   A. 1990 - *Black Velvet* B. 1977 - *Black Is Black*
   C. 1974 - *The Black-Eyed Boys*

3. Excluding Henry Cooper, name the three British boxers who fought Muhammed Ali.

4. In the TV series *Cats Eyes* which three actresses played the crime-fighting trio?

5. Which are the three most common types of cloud?

6. Name the last films of the following stars. A. John Wayne
   B. Marilyn Monroe C. Steve McQueen

7. In bingo slang what numbers are represented by the following phrases? A. Kelly's eye B. The Brighton line C. Sunset Strip

8. In the *Magic Roundabout* what is the name of the A. Dog
   B. Cow C. Rabbit?

9. On whose novels are the following TV programmes based?
   A. *Inspector Morse* B. *Rumpole of the Bailey* C. *Little House on the Prairie*

10. What are the names of the farms in A. *Animal Farm* B. *Worzel Gummidge* C. *The Archers*?

ANSWERS

1. David Jacobs, Noel Edmonds & Jools Holland 2. A. Alannah Myles B. La Belle Epoque C. Paper Lace 3. Brian London, Joe Bugner & Richard Dunn 4. Jill Gascoine, Leslie Ash & Rosalyn Landor 5. Nimbus, cumulus & cirrus 6. A. The Shootist B. The Misfits C. The Hunter 7. A. 1 B. 59 C. 77 8. A. Dougal B. Ermintrude C. Dylan 9. A. Colin Dexter B. John Mortimer C. Laura Ingalls Wilder 10. A. Manor Farm B. Scatterbrook Farm C. Brookfield Farm

QUIZ EIGHT

1. Alpha, Bravo, Charlie. What are the next three?

2. What were the Beatles' first three UK No. 1 hits?

3. What are the first names of the three Wallace brothers who played together for Southampton FC in 1988?

4. In *Cagney & Lacey* name the three actresses who have played Christine Cagney.

5. On the first day of Christmas my true love gave to me a partridge in a pear tree. What gifts came on the 10th, 11th and 12th days?

6. What are the names of the three female murder suspects in *Cluedo*?

7. What three books follow Genesis in the Bible?

8. Name the three actors that accompanied George Peppard in *The A Team*.

9. Which three actresses married the film director John Derek?

10. What are the first names of the rock trio Emerson, Lake & Palmer?

ANSWERS

1. Delta, Echo & Foxtrot. 2. 'From Me To You', 'She Loves You' & 'I Want To Hold Your Hand' 3. Rod, Ray & Danny 4. Loretta Swit, Meg Foster, Sharon Gless 5. 10 pipers piping, 11 ladies dancing & 12 lords a leaping 6. Mrs White, Mrs Peacock & Miss Scarlet 7. Exodus, Leviticus & Numbers 8. Dwight Schulz, Dirk Benedict & Mr T 9. Ursula Andress, Linda Evans & Bo Derek 10. Keith, Greg & Carl

QUIZ NINE

1. What are the names of the newspapers in A. *Superman* B. *Hot Metal* C. *Citizen Kane*?

2. In what year did the following people die? A. Queen Victoria B. Winston Churchill C. John Lennon

3. On which island was Napoleon Bonaparte A. Born B. Died C. Exiled?

4. Name the three actor members of the original Magnificent Seven whose surname began with the letter B.

5. What are the first names of the following detectives? A. Bergerac B. Van Der Valk C. Miss Marple

6. In which countries are the following Shakespeare plays set? A. *Hamlet* B. *Macbeth* C. *Romeo and Juliet*

7. What are the three operative words on a Ouija board?

8. What are the heraldic names for the following colours? A. Black B. Red C. Green

9. What are the occupations of the literary Three Men In A Tub?

10. Which DJ's have the following nicknames? A. Stewpot B. The hairy monster C. Fluff

QUIZ TEN

1. Who were the first three Presidents of the USA?
2. Name the team captains and the host of 'Have I Got News For You?'
3. What are the middle names of the following politicians?
   A. Richard Nixon B. Margaret Thatcher C. Neil Kinnock
4. Other than Mercury what are the three surnames of the pop group Queen?
5. Who were the first three Labour Prime Ministers in Britain?
6. Who were the first three actors to play James Bond?
7. Name the three pop star husbands of Patsy Kensit.
8. What are the names of Queen Elizabeth II's three eldest grandchildren?
9. Name the three men who were founder members of the SDP.
10. What are the names of the three sons of the biblical Noah?

ANSWERS

1. Washington, Adams & Jefferson 2. Paul Merton, Ian Hislop & Angus Deayton
3. A. Milhouse B. Hilda C. Gordon 4. Deacon, May & Taylor 5. Ramsay Macdonald, Clement Attlee & Harold Wilson 6. Sean Connery, David Niven & George Lazenby
7. Liam Gallagher, Jim Kerr & Dan Donavon 8. William, Peter & Zara 9. Roy Jenkins, David Owen & Bill Rodgers 10. Shem, Ham & Japeth

QUIZ ONE

1. Name the three actresses who on film formed The First Wives' Club.

2. Name the artists who sang the following songs for the UK in the Eurovision Song Contest A. 'Ooh Ahh Just A Little Bit' B. 'Let Me Be The One' C. 'One Step Further'.

3. Name the three horses who finished the 2001 Grand National, behind the winner Red Marauder.

4. Excluding the hurdle race, over what three distances are the track events run in a men's decathlon?

5. In the American soap *Dallas* what three surnames did Miss Ellie have?

6. Who played Frankenstein's monster in the following films?
A. 1957-*The Curse of Frankenstein* B. 1974 - *Frankenstein The True Story* C. 1974 - *Young Frankenstein*.

7. In which countries did the following food originate?
A. Chutney B. Tabasco sauce C. Chop suey

8. Who were the first three British groups to have a No. 1 hit single in the USA?

9. Which cities are overlooked by the following mountains?
A. Sugar Loaf Mountain B. Table Mountain C. Mount Everest

10. In the 1967 film *Bonnie & Clyde* who played A. Bonnie Parker B. Clyde Barrow C. Buck Barrow?

QUIZ TWO

1. In *The Flintstones* what is the name of A. Fred's wife B. Fred's hometown C. The Flintstones' family pet?

2. Who wrote about the following doctors? A. Dr Zhivago B. Dr Doolittle C. Dr Faustus

3. Name the 'yellow' hits of the following recording artists. A. Joni Mitchell B. Donovan C. Dawn

4. In the 1960s which golfers were known as The Big Three?

5. In the famous children's story what did each of the three little pigs use to build their houses?

6. What are the titles of the first three films to feature the character of Indiana Jones?

7. In radio terminology what do the following initials stand for? A. CB B. VHF C. MW

8. Name the actors who played The Good, the Bad and the Ugly.

9. Who are the lead singers of the following pop groups? A. Catatonia B. Generation X C. Led Zeppelin

10. What would be your star sign if you were born on A. Christmas Day B. Halloween C. April Fool's Day?

ANSWERS

1. A. Wilma B. Bedrock C. Dino 2. A. Boris Pasternak B. Hugh Lofting C. Thomas Mann 3. A. 'Big Yellow Taxi' B. 'Mellow Yellow' C. 'Tie A Yellow Ribbon Round The Old Oak Tree' 4. Jack Nicklaus, Arnold Palmer & Gary Player 5. Straw, sticks & bricks 6. *Raiders of the Lost Ark*, *Indiana Jones and The Temple of Doom* & *Indiana Jones and the Last Crusade* 7. A. Citizen's Band B. Very High Frequency C. Medium Wave 8. Clint Eastwood, Lee Van Cleef & Eli Wallach 9. A. Cerys Matthews B. Billy Idol C. Robert Plant 10. A. Capricorn B. Scorpio C. Aries.

27

QUIZ THREE

1. In the film *Pulp Fiction* who played A. Vincent B. Mia C. Jules?

2. What are the first three letters on a typewriter keyboard?

3. In the English flat racing season which three Classics comprise the Triple Crown?

4. What were the titles of the three films that Morecambe & Wise made together?

5. There are four words beginning with the letter C that are used to describe the quality of a diamond. One is colour, name the other three.

6. What are the mottos of the following organizations? A. SAS B. Boy Scouts C. Salvation Army

7. What are known as the three kingdoms of nature?

8. What are the three Cardinal Virtues?

9. Which actresses of yesteryear were known by the following nicknames? A. The Legs B. The Sweater Girl C. The Brazilian Bombshell

10. Which words ending with "ore" describe the following? A. Meat-eating animal B. Plant-eating animal C. An animal that eats meat and plants

QUIZ FOUR

1. What three colours are featured on the Italian flag?

2. Solomon Grundy was born on a Monday. What happened to him on Tuesday, Wednesday & Thursday?

3. Name the only three films that featured James Dean in a starring role.

4. How many are in a A. Baker's dozen B. Score C. Gross?

5. What were the first UK No. 1 hits of the following pop groups? A. The Police B. Madness C. Queen

6. In the 1980s which three British athletes held the world record for the mile?

7. What type of wood are the following traditionally made from? A. Chippendale furniture B. Cricket bats C. Rolls Royce dashboards

8. In the film *Mary Poppins* who played A. Mary B. Bert C. Mr Banks?

9. In a game of Scrabble what is the points value of A. The letter Z B. The letter K C. The letter C?

10. What are the first names of the Beverley Sisters?

QUIZ FIVE

....

IN TERMS OF POPULATION WHAT ARE THE THREE LARGEST CITIES IN THE FOLLOWING LIST OF COUNTRIES?

1. Australia
2. Canada
3. France
4. India
5. The Republic of Ireland
6. New Zealand
7. Norway
8. Spain
9. Sweden
10. Turkey

ANSWERS

1. Sydney, Melbourne & Brisbane   2. Toronto, Montreal & Vancouver   3. Paris, Lyon &
Marseille   4. Bombay, Calcutta & Delhi   5. Dublin, Cork & Limerick   6. Auckland,
Wellington & Christchurch   7. Oslo, Bergen & Trondheim   8. Madrid, Barcelona & Valencia
9. Stockholm, Gothenburg & Malmo   10. Istanbul, Ankara & Izmir

QUIZ SIX

1. Who played M in the following Bond films? A. *Goldeneye*
   B. *Moonraker* C. *Never Say Never Again*

2. Who were the first three men to actually set foot on the moon?

3. In what year did the following TV channels broadcast for the
   first time? A. BBC 2 B. Channel 5 C. Channel 4

4. The following English football teams all moved to new grounds
   in the 1990s. Name their new grounds. A. Huddersfield
   B. Derby County C. Middlesborough

5. What were the best-selling singles in the UK in each of the last
   three decades of the 20th century?

6. In a clockwise direction which three numbers follow 20 on
   a dartboard?

7. Who is credited with inventing the A. Telephone B. Television
   C. Telescope?

8. Who composed the following operas? A. *Madam Butterfly*
   B. *Aida* C. *Carmen*

9. Which pop groups with the word 'New' in their name hit the
   charts with the following songs? A. 'I'd Like To Teach The World
   To Sing' B. 'Blue Monday' C. 'Candy Girl'

10. Name the Disney characters that sang the following songs on
    film. A. 'Bare Necessities' B. 'When You Wish Upon A Star'
    C. 'Whistle While You Work'

QUIZ SEVEN

1. The JCB was named after the initials of its inventor. What do those initials stand for?

2. Who are the three members of the pop trio the Scaffold?

3. In 1995 Oasis became the fourth pop group beginning with the letter O to top the UK singles charts. Who were the previous three?

4. Name the three No. 1 hit singles of Bucks Fizz.

5. Name the three West Ham United footballers who played for England in the 1966 World Cup Final.

6. Alphabetically what are the last three American states?

7. In the sitcom *Birds of a Feather* who played A. Sharon B. Tracy C. Dorien?

8. Which football teams do the following pop stars support?
   A. Liam Gallagher B. Mel C C. Robbie Williams

9. In the Rocky films name the actors who played the following boxers. A. Ivan Drago B. Clubber Lang C. Apollo Creed

10. In which English county would you find the following?
   A. Penzance B. Jodrell Bank C. Skegness

QUIZ EIGHT

1. What are the names of the three types of sword used in fencing?

2. What are the first names of the Kray brothers?

3. Which cities do the following baseball teams come from?
   A. The Pirates B. The Cardinals C. The Orioles

4. What are the three most common surnames in Britain?

5. What are the names of the schools that featured in?
   A. *Fame* B. *Billy Bunter* C. *The Prime of Miss Jean Brodie*

6. What are the three winter months in the southern hemisphere?

7. In the film *Saving Private Ryan* who played A. Private Ryan
   B. Captain Miller C. Captain Hammil?

8. What are the three primary colours?

9. What name is given to an animal that A. Chews cud
   B. Carries its young in a pouch C. Possesses hooves?

10. Name the three actors to have played the Blues Brothers on film.

QUIZ NINE

1. Name the three members of the International Olympic Committee that were not invited to the 1948 Summer Olympics.

2. What are the surnames of A. Boy George B. The Great Soprendo C. The Krankies?

3. What three words of Japanese origin when translated into English mean A. Divine wind B. Empty hand C. Empty orchestra?

4. Which fruits form the base for the following drinks? A. Cider B. Cointreau C. Grenadine

5. Name the countries that hosted football's World Cup in the following years. A. 1958 B. 1970 C. 1978

6. What sort of bird is the symbol of A. Wisdom B. Peace C. Happiness?

7. Bjorn Borg beat four different opponents when winning his Wimbledon titles. John McEnroe was one, name the other three.

8. What is the largest A. Japanese island B. Caribbean island C. Greek island?

9. Who was known as A. The father of medicine B. The father of trigonometry C. The father of geometry?

10. What are the first three words in the Bible?

QUIZ TEN

1. In the sitcom *Friends* what are the character names of the three female friends?

2. Name the three men who made up the Goodies.

3. Name the three men who hosted the game show *The Wheel of Fortune* in the 20th century.

4. As played by Barbara Knox in *Coronation Street* what were the first three surnames of Rita?

5. In *Last of the Summer Wine* who played A. Compo B. Clegg C. Foggy?

6. Name the three presenters who accompanied Jeremy Beadle in the very first edition of *Game For A Laugh*.

7. In *Till Death Us Do Part* who played A. Alf Garnett B. Rita C. Else?

8. Name the three actresses who were the original Charlie's Angels on TV.

9. Name the three non-human characters that accompanied Geoffrey Hayes on the children's TV show *Rainbow*.

10. In which soaps would you meet the following characters? A. Joe Mangel B. Ray Krebbs C. Matt Wilson

SESSION 4

QUIZ ONE

1. Name the three duos that had a hit with the song 'You're The One That I Want' from the musical *Grease*.

2. In which newspapers would you read the following cartoon strips? A. Andy Capp B. Rupert the Bear C. Beau Peep

3. In the sitcom *Are You Being Served?* who played A. Mr Humphries B. Miss Brahms C. Mr Lucas?

4. Which film company's initials are MGM?

5. What were the surnames of the three West Indian cricketers who were collectively known as "The Three W's"?

6. Who were the Vice-Presidents of A. Bill Clinton B. John F Kennedy C. Jimmy Carter?

7. In which century were the following buildings built? A. Eiffel Tower B. Taj Mahal C. Westminster Abbey

8. In which three consecutive years did Fred Perry win the Wimbledon Singles Title?

9. *In The Professionals* who played Bodie, Doyle and Cowley?

10. Who wrote the following 'virginal' books? A. *The Virgin Soldiers* B. *Losing My Virginity* C. *The Virgin And The Gypsy*

QUIZ TWO

1. Which three pop group members followed Dave Dee and Dozy?

2. In which European cities could you visit the following attractions? A. The Luxembourg Gardens B. The Trevi Fountain C. The Tivoli Gardens

3. Name the No. I hits for the following artists that contain the word "everything" in the title of the song. A. Bryan Adams B. Boy George C. The Real Thing

4. What were the first three novels of Charles Dickens?

5. What were the first three years that Brazil won football's World Cup?

6. What were the names of the dogs in A. *Dr Who* B. *Hart to Hart* C. *Beverly Hillbillies*?

7. Name the three people that hosted the quiz show *A Question of Sport* in the 20th century.

8. What are the first names of the Bronte sisters?

9. What three flavours makeup Neapolitan ice cream?

10. What names are given to a male, female and young swan?

QUIZ THREE

1. Who were the three founder members of The Who that remained after the death of Keith Moon?

2. Who were the first footballer, first actor and first jockey to be knighted?

3. What are the top ranks in the Army, RAF and Navy?

4. Who played the leading ladies in the following films?
   A. *Casablanca* B. *Top Gun* C. *Butch Cassidy and the Sundance Kid*.

5. Which TV series of yesteryear was set in the following locations?
   A. Wameru Study Centre B. Altdorf C. Marineville

6. Who won the Oxford and Cambridge boat race in A. 1999 B. 2000 C. 1877?

7. What is the favourite food of the following characters?
   A. Popeye B. Desperate Dan C. The Teenage Mutant Ninja Turtles

8. Which three suits accompany pentacles in a pack of Tarot cards?

9. Name the three men that founded the United Artists Film Company with Mary Pickford.

10. What is Austria's A. Capital city B. National flower C. Currency?

QUIZ FOUR

1. Name the films that featured the following rival gangs.
   A. The Jets and the Sharks B. The Beetles and the Black Rebels
   C. The Faces and the Barracudas

2. Name the actors who play Joey, Chandler and Ross in the sitcom *Friends*.

3. What are the three largest islands in the Arctic Ocean?

4. What were the names of the first three Popes?

5. How many squares are there on a A. Scrabble board
   B. Chess board C. Monopoly board?

6. After whom were America, Bolivia and Rhodesia named?

7. Name the pop groups that had hits with the following songs concerning the moon. A. 'Man On The Moon' B. 'Whole Of The Moon' C. 'Bad Moon Rising'

8. In the sitcom *Hi-de-hi* who played Gladys, Spike and Peggy?

9. What sort of creatures were the following literary creations?
   A. Rikki Tikki Tavi B. Shardik C. Captain Flint

10. Dragon, dog, chicken, monkey, snake, tiger, pig, sheep and rat.
    Which three other animals comprise the Chinese calendar?

ANSWERS

1. A. *West Side Story* B. *The Wild One* C. *Saturday Night Fever* 2. Matt le Blanc, Matthew Perry and David Schwimmer 3. Greenland, Baffin Island & Ellesmere Island 4. Peter, Linus & Cletus – who was also known as Anacletus 5. A. 225 B. 64 C. 40 6. Amerigo Vespucchi, Simon Bolivar & Cecil Rhodes 7. A. REM B. The Waterboys C. Creedence Clearwater Revival 8. Ruth Madoc, Jeffrey Holland & Su Pollard 9. A. Mongoose B. Bear C. Parrot 10. Horse, rabbit & ox

QUIZ FIVE

1. What are the three ingredients of a Harvey Wallbanger cocktail?

2. Which three vegetables belong to the classification of brassica oleracae along with cauliflower and cabbage?

3. What sort of fruits are the following? A. Bartlett B. Honeydew C. Victoria

4. Which drinks have been advertised on TV by the following people? A. Leonard Rossiter & Joan Collins B. Sharon Maughan & Anthony Head C. Ian Wright & Denise Van Outen

5. How many bottles of champagne are in a A. Jeroboam B. Salmanazar C. Nebuchadnezzar?

6. What are the national dishes of the following countries? A. Greece B. Spain C. Hungary

7. Which recording artists with a fruity sounding name had hits with the following songs? A. 1968 - 'Green Tambourine' B. 1979 - 'Reunited' C. 1986 - 'Every Loser Wins'

8. Name the chocolate bars that are advertised on TV with the following slogans. A. Full of Eastern promise B. The taste of paradise C. It's that Friday feeling

9. From which countries do the following wines originate? A. Asti Spumante B. Moselle C. Vinho Verde

10. What are the three ingredients of a Pina Colada cocktail?

ANSWERS

1. Vodka, galliano & orange juice 2. Kale, broccoli & brussels sprouts 3. A. Pear B. Melon C. Plum 4. A. Cinzano B. Gold Blend C. Nescafe 5. A. 4 B. 12 C. 20 6. A. Moussaka B. Paella C. Goulash 7. A. Lemon Pipers B. Peaches & Herb C. Nick Berry 8. A. Turkish Delight B. Bounty C. Crunchie 9. A. Italy B. Germany C. Portugal 10. Rum, pineapple juice & coconut milk

QUIZ SIX

1. What are the three longest rivers in Scotland?

2. Name the first three actors to play the Bond villain Blofeld on film.

3. Name the first three recording artists to have a UK chart hit with the song 'I Believe'.

4. Name the three actors who played the long-term hospital patients in the sitcom *Only When I Laugh*.

5. Which were the first three countries in the world to issue postage stamps?

6. Between 1950 and the year 2000 which three Scots managed Manchester United?

7. In which three films did Michael Caine play the character of Harry Palmer?

8. What are the medical names for the three bones in the ear?

9. In the film *Shakespeare in Love* who played A. Shakespeare B. Lord Wessex C. Queen Elizabeth?

10. What are the names of Hyacinth's three sisters in the sitcom *Keeping Up Appearances?*

QUIZ SEVEN

1. Name the footballers who wrote the following autobiographies.
   A. *Rock Bottom* B. *Psycho* C. *Addicted*

2. 'Monday's child is fair of face, Tuesday's child is full of grace.' How are the children described in the next three days?

3. Peter Sellers was married four times. One of his wives was Anne Hayes, name the other three.

4. Name Clint Eastwood's leading ladies in the following films.
   A. *The Enforcer* B. *In The Line Of Fire* C. *Two Mules For Sister Sarah*

5. Who were the first three French footballers to be voted European Footballer of the Year?

6. With which three pop groups did Roy Wood enjoy top 10 hits in the 1960s and 70s?

7. Name the three entertainers who presented the talent show *Opportunity Knocks* in the 20th century.

8. In *Upstairs, Downstairs* who played Thomas, Sarah & Hudson?

9. What are the three largest Channel Islands?

10. The song 'Unchained Melody' became the first song to be a No. 1 hit for three different artists. Name the artists in question.

QUIZ EIGHT

1. John F Kennedy became the fourth US President to be assassinated. What are the surnames of the other three?

2. In computer terminology what three words are represented by the initials WWW?

3. Name the three English football league clubs whose name ends in Athletic.

4. What were the first three non European cities to host the Summer Olympics?

5. What sort of creatures were the following film and book characters? A. Mighty Joe Young B. My Friend Flicka C. Old Yeller

6. Who were the first three cricketers to play 100 test matches for England?

7. Name the actors that committed the murders in the following films. A. *The Boston Strangler* B. *A Nightmare On Elm Street* C. *Kind Hearts and Coronets*

8. There are four graded horse-racing courses in England whose name ends with the letter Y. One is Wetherby, name the other three.

9. How are the following pop stars better known? A. Terry Nelhams B. Marshall Mathers C. Doug Trendel

10. Who assassinated the following people? A. John Lennon B. Lee Harvey Oswald C. Martin Luther King

---

ANSWERS

1. Lincoln, Garfield & McKinley 2. World Wide Web 3. Oldham, Wigan & Charlton 4. 1904 - St Louis, 1932 - Los Angeles & 1956 - Melbourne 5. A. Gorilla B. Horse C. Dog 6. Colin Cowdrey, Geoffrey Boycott & David Gower 7. A. Tony Curtis B. Robert England C. Dennis Price 8. Beverley, Salisbury & Newbury 9. A. Adam Faith B. Eminem C. Buster Bloodvessel 10. A. Mark Chapman B. Jack Ruby C. James Earl Ray

QUIZ NINE

1. Who scored the only goal in the following FA Cup Finals?
   A. 1995 - Everton 1 Manchester United 0 B. 1973 - Sunderland
   1 Leeds United 0 C. 1985 - Manchester United 1 Everton 0.

2. In which TV series did David Jason play A. Skullion B. Granville
   C. Blanco?

3. In which cities would you find the following bridges? A. Rialto
   B. Golden Gate C. Howrah

4. Which parts of the human body are affected by the following
   diseases? A. Dermatitis B. Otitis C. Glossitis

5. Name the wives of A. Roger Rabbit B. Babar the Elephant
   C. Fungus the Bogeyman.

6. In which films did the following actors make their debut as James
   Bond? A. Timothy Dalton B. Roger Moore C. Pierce Brosnan

7. Which organizations did the following TV characters work for?
   A. Captain Scarlet B. Napoleon Solo C. The Champions

8. Who were the first three female singers to have No. 1 hits in
   the UK before their 17th birthday?

9. Name the three actresses who played office work colleagues in
   the film *9 to 5*.

10. Who is the patron saint of A. Policemen B. Lovers
    C. Germany?

ANSWERS

1. A. Paul Rideout B. Ian Porterfield C. Norman Whiteside 2. A. Porterhouse Blues
B. Open All Hours C. Porridge 3. A. Venice B. San Francisco C. Calcutta 4. A. Skin
B. Ear C. Tongue 5. A. Jessica B. Celeste C. Mildew 6. A. The Living Daylights
B. Live and Let Die C. Goldeneye 7. A. Spectrum B. UNCLE C. Nemesis 8. Helen Shapiro,
Tiffany & Billie Piper 9. Dolly Parton, Jane Fonda & Lily Tomlin 10. A. Michael
B. Valentine C. Boniface

44

QUIZ TEN

1. Which three England football managers appeared together in a TV ad for Yellow Pages in 1994?
2. Which three Scottish league clubs has Alex Ferguson managed?
3. Name the three Dutch clubs who won the European Cup in the 20th century.
4. Which three Scottish grounds staged finals of European club competitions in the 20th century?
5. Brian Clough managed both Derby County and Nottingham Forest to league titles. Which other three clubs did he manage?
6. Which were the first three British clubs to win the European Cup?
7. Which were the first three post-war goalkeepers to captain England?
8. What are the 'bird' nicknames of A. West Bromich Albion B. Cardiff City C. Norwich City.
9. Which three nations won football's World Cup in the 1990s?
10. Which football clubs had hit records with A. 'The Anfield Rap' B. 'Blue is the Colour' C. 'Ossie's Dream'?

ANSWERS

1. Graham Taylor, Terry Venables & Bobby Robson 2. Aberdeen, St Mirren & East Stirling 3. Ajax, Feyenoord & PSV Eindhoven 4. Hampden Park, Ibrox Park & Tannadice 5. Leeds, Hartlepool & Brighton 6. Manchester United, Celtic & Liverpool 7. Frank Swift, Ray Clemence & Peter Shilton 8. A. The Throstles B. The Bluebirds C. The Canaries 9. France, Brazil & West Germany 10. A. Liverpool B. Chelsea C. Tottenham

QUIZ ONE

1. Who played the title roles in the following films? A. *Peggy Sue Got Married* B. *The Elephant Man* C. *Jerry Maguire*

2. What was the maiden name of A. Margaret Thatcher B. Evonne Cawley C. Agatha Christie?

3. Which wars witnessed the following conflicts? A. Charge of the Light Brigade B. The Battle of the Somme C. The Battle of Marengo

4. Name the women writers of the following books. A. *The Female Eunuch* B. *Polo* C. *The Thorn Birds*

5. What were the food, drink and home of the Greek Gods?

6. Who did David Bowie collaborate with on the following songs? A. 'Under Pressure' B. 'Dancing In The Street' C. 'Little Drummer Boy'

7. In which cities are the following TV programmes set? A. *Friends* B. *Dynasty* C. *Casualty*

8. Which groups released the following albums? A. *Brothers In Arms* B. *Parklife* C. *The Joshua Tree*

9. In the Simon & Garfunkel song 'Scarborough Fair' which three herbs follow parsley in the lyrics of the song?

10. What are the secret identities of A. The Incredible Hulk B. Batman C. Spiderman

QUIZ TWO

1. How many players are there in a A. Netball team B. Australian Rules football team C. Rugby Union team?

2. What are the following ologies the study of? A. Pomology B. Cryptology C. Petrology

3. What are the real first names of? A. Coco Chanel B. Groucho Marx C. Babe Ruth

4. The following three recording artists all had No. 1 hit singles, the titles of which all began with the letter B. Name the three songs. A. Sweet B. Art Garfunkel C. Cher

5. What is the name of the dog in the following? A. *The Perishers* cartoon strip B. *The Wacky Races* C. On the HMV record label.

6. Which sci-fi films were based on the following novels? A. *Do Androids Dream of Electric Sheep?* B. *The Sentinel* C. *Monkey Planet*

7. In which cartoon series did the following characters appear? A. Vincent Van Gopher B. Klunk C. Mr Peevley, the zoo warden

8. Who created the following literary 'Harrys'? A. Harry Palmer B. Harry Potter C. Harry Lime

9. In the sitcom *Absolutely Fabulous* who played Saffron, Edina & Bubble?

10. What do the following Cockney rhyming slang expressions stand for? A. April showers B. Hampstead Heath C. Jam jar

ANSWERS
1. A. 7 B. 18 C. 15 2. A. Fruit B. Codes 3. A. Gabrielle B. Julius C. George
4. A. Blockbuster B. Bright Eyes C. Believe 5. A. Boot B. Muttley C. Nipper
6. A. Bladerunner B. 2001-A Space Odyssey C. Planet of the Apes 7. A. Deputy Dawg
B. Stop the Pigeon C. The Hair Bear Bunch 8. A. Len Deighton B. JK Rowling
C. Graham Greene 9. Julia Sawalha, Jennifer Saunders & Jane Horrocks 10. A. Flowers
B. Teeth C. Car

5

QUIZ THREE

1. What three animals are mentioned in the nursery rhyme 'Hey diddle diddle'?

2. What are the theme songs of? A. The Harlem Globetrotters B. Bob Hope C. West Ham United FC

3. What do Americans call A. Curtains B. The boot of a car C. Pavement?

4. What nationality were A. Aladdin B. El Cid C. William Tell?

5. What nicknames were given to the following criminals? A. Robert F Stroud B. David Berkowitz C. John George Haig

6. In the TV sketch show *Three of a Kind* which entertainers made up the three?

7. Which cities are nicknamed A. The Eternal City B. The Granite City C. The Windy City?

8. What is the more common name for A. Calcium carbonate B. Acetic acid C. Ethylene glycol?

9. Which towns or cities did the Romans call A. Dubris B. Deva C. Clausentum?

10. In the sitcom *Frasier* who plays Frasier Crane, Niles Crane & Martin Crane?

QUIZ FOUR

1. What is the more common name for the following diseases?
   A. Pertussis B. Varicella C. Herpes Zoster

2. In which American cities do the following basketball teams play?
   A. The Bulls B. The Supersonics C. The Celtics

3. What are the best-selling daily newspapers in A. UK B. USA
   C. Canada?

4. Which countries did the following winning artists represent in
   the Eurovision Song Contest? A. Nicole B. Sandra Kim
   C. Dana International

5. Who were the first three British drivers to be Formula One
   World Champion on four wheels?

6. Which three kings sat on the British throne during the
   19th century?

7. Name the three men who led the Conservative Party during
   the 1960s.

8. What is the highest mountain in A. Scotland B. England
   C. Wales?

9. Who played Billy the Kid in the following films? A. 1958 - *The
   Left Handed Gun* B. 1973 - *Pat Garrett and Billy the Kid*
   C. 1950 - *Texas Kid Outlaw*

10. What are the capital cities, beginning with the letter A, of the
    following countries? A. Greece B. Ethiopia C. Ghana

ANSWERS

1. A. Whooping cough B. Chickenpox C. Shingles 2. A. Chicago B. Seattle C. Boston
3. A. *The Sun* B. *The Wall St Journal* C. *The Toronto Star* 4. A. Germany B. Belgium
C. Israel 5. Mike Hawthorn, Graham Hill & Jim Clark 6. George III, George IV and
William IV 7. Harold Macmillan, Alec Douglas-Hume and Edward Heath 8. A. Ben Nevis
B. Scafell Pike C. Snowdon 9. A. Paul Newman B. Kris Kristofferson C. Audie Murphy
10. A. Athens B. Addis Ababa C. Accra

QUIZ FIVE

....

1. What is the country of origin of the following car manufacturers?
   A. Saab B. Lancia C. Seat

2. What are the titles of the three sequels to *The Love Bug* featuring the Volkswagen called Herbie?

3. Where did the following pop groups catch a train to in a song?
   A. The Monkees B. ELO C. Gladys Knight and the Pips

4. Which cities are served by the following airports? A. Orly
   B. O'Hare C. Bromma

5. Who is credited with inventing A. The car B. The hovercraft
   C. The motor bike?

6. In which TV programmes did the following sailing vessels feature?
   A. *Charlotte Rhodes* B. *Pacific Princess* C. *Vital Spark*

7. Which recording artists had a hit with? A. 1979 - 'Cars'
   B. 1982 - 'Driving In My Car' C. 1988 - 'Get Outta My Dreams Get Into My Car'

8. Which British cities are served by the following railway stations?
   A. New Street B. Temple Meads C. Waverley

9. What are the names of the national airlines of A. Hong Kong
   B. Ireland C. Portugal?

10. After London what were the first three British cities to have an underground railway system?

QUIZ SIX

1. Name the three women who were the BBC's Sports Personality of the Year in the 1970s.

2. What are the three busiest airports in the UK?

3. In which countries did the following dances originate? A. Bossa Nova B. Rumba C. Mazurka

4. What are the national birds of A. New Zealand B. USA C. India?

5. What were the last three decades in which Halley's Comet was seen from Earth?

6. Who played A. Tarzan in 12 films B. Mr Moto in 8 films C. Sherlock Holmes in 14 films?

7. Who piloted *Thunderbird 1*, *Thunderbird 2* and *Thunderbird 3* respectively?

8. What names did Sigmund Freud give to the three main divisions of the human psyche?

9. Jay, Donny and Jimmy. Name the three missing Osmond Brothers.

10. Who are the Three Tenors?

ANSWERS

1. Virginia Wade, Mary Peters & Princess Anne 2. Heathrow, Manchester & Gatwick 3. A. Brazil B. Cuba C. Poland 4. A. Kiwi B. Bald Eagle C. Peacock 5. 1980s, 1910s and 1830s 6. A. Johnny Weismuller B. Peter Lorre C. Basil Rathbone 7. Scott, Virgil and Alan 8. The ego, super ego and the id 9. Wayne, Merrill and Alan 10. Luciano Pavarotti, Placido Domingo and José Carreras

QUIZ SEVEN

1. Which three American states have a P in their name?
2. What are the names of the three Gabor sisters?
3. What are the nationalities of the following former World Formula One Champions? A. Alain Prost B. Mario Andretti C. Niki Lauda
4. Which Shakespeare plays were the following films based upon? A. *West Side Story* B. *Kiss Me Kate* C. Akiro Kurosawa's *Ran*
5. Who was the first member of the Royal Family to A. Graduate from university B. Appear as a guest on a TV quiz show C. Sue a newspaper?
6. On which courses are the following run? A. Scottish Grand National B. English Grand National C. Welsh Grand National
7. Who were the first three boxers to beat Muhammed Ali professionally?
8. What are the names of the three female members of the Corrs?
9. In the sitcom *Rising Damp* who played A. Rigsby B. Miss Jones C. Phillip?
10. What are the three most easterly English football teams in the football league?

QUIZ EIGHT

1. What are the nationalities of the following Tour de France winners? A. Eddy Merckx B. Greg Le Mond C. Miguel Indurain

2. Name the three actors that played the three Geordie characters in *Auf Wiedersehen Pet*.

3. In which years were the following people born? A. Macauley Culkin B. Nick Berry C. Sheena Easton

4. Between 1960 and the year 2000 which three male tennis players won four or more Wimbledon Singles titles?

5. What were the names of the singing chipmunks who had a hit with 'Ragtime Cowboy Joe'?

6. In which film did Robin Williams play A. Daniel Hillard B. John Keating C. Peter Banning?

7. What are the names of the three children of the actor Sir John Mills?

8. What are the names of the three members of the pop group the Jam?

9. What were the first three countries to launch a rocket into space?

10. In which TV programmes do the following catchphrases appear? A. 'Come on Down' B. 'Book 'em Danno' C. 'Nothing in this game for two in a bed'

ANSWERS

1. A. Belgian B. American C. Spanish 2. Kevin Whately, Tim Healy & Jimmy Nail 3. A. 1980 B. 1963 C. 1959 4. Bjorn Borg, Pete Sampras & Rod Laver 5. Alvin, Theodore & Simon 6. A. Mrs Doubtfire B. Dead Poets Society C. Hook 7. Juliet, Hayley & Jonathan 8. Paul Weller, Bruce Foxton & Rick Buckler 9. USA, USSR & France 10. A. The Price Is Right B. Hawaii 5–0 C. Bullseye

QUIZ NINE

1. At the 2001 Oscar ceremonies, who received the award for A. Best Actor B. Best Actress C. Best Director?

2. What is the capital city of A. Chile B. El Salvador C. Costa Rica?

3. What are the names of the three main male characters in the TV series *Cold Feet*?

4. Which American states are nicknamed A. The Nutmeg State B. The Mormon State C. The Lone Star State?

5. What were the surnames of the three husbands of Marilyn Monroe?

6. On TV who played the female half of A. *George & Mildred* B. *Dempsey & Makepiece* C. *The Scarecrow and Mrs King*

7. Who were the first three singers to have a UK hit with the song 'My Way'?

8. Who were the first three Swedish groups to have a No. 1 hit in the UK?

9. From which clubs did Arsenal FC sign A. Ian Wright B. David Seaman C. Dennis Bergkamp?

10. Name the three men in the original line up of the pop group Bros.

QUIZ TEN

1. On which three Shakespeare plays did the composer Verdi base operas?

2. What are the names of the three Darling children in *Peter Pan*?

3. Which three 20th-century novels featured the character of Hannibal Lecter?

4. Who wrote the following 'Lord' novels? A. *Lord of the Flies* B. *Lord of the Rings* C. *Lord Jim*

5. What are the first names of the following literary characters? A. Dr Jeckyll B. Baron Frankenstein C. Lady Chatterley

6. What are the names of King Lear's three daughters?

7. What are the names of the first three Harry Potter books?

8. In *Winnie the Pooh* what are the names of the donkey, the elephant and the joey?

9. Who wrote the following novels? A. *The Day of the Jackal* B. *The Day of the Triffids* C. *The Day of the Locust*

10. What are the titles of the first three novels in the *Narnia Chronicles*?

ANSWERS

1. Othello, Macbeth & The Merry Wives of Windsor 2. Wendy, Michael & John 3. Silence of the Lambs, Hannibal & Red Dragon 4. A. William Golding B. JRR Tolkien C. Joseph Conrad 5. A. Henry B. Victor C. Constance 6. Goneril, Regan & Cordelia 7. Harry Potter and the Philosopher's Stone, Harry Potter and the Chamber of Secrets & Harry Potter and the Prisoner of Azkaban 8. Eeyore, Heffalump & Roo 9. A. Frederick Forsythe B. John Wyndham C. Nathanael West 10. The Magician's Nephew, The Lion, the Witch and the Wardrobe & The Horse and his Boy

QUIZ ONE

1. What are the names of the three female members of Enid Blyton's Secret Seven?

2. Which TV programmes featured the following teachers?
   A. Mrs McCluskey B. Miss Titley C. Principal Skinner

3. Who were the first three men with the surname of Hill to have a solo top 10 hit single in the UK?

4. In the 2000 film *Space Cowboys* name the three actors who co-starred with Clint Eastwood as astronauts brought out of retirement for one final mission.

5. Name the three Charleses who wrote the following books.
   A. *The Water Babies* B. *The Origin of Species* C. *Elementary Seismology*

6. What three colours of jersey are awarded during the Tour de France?

7. Which 'feline' recording artists had hits with A. 'Down to Earth' B. 'Moonshadow' C. 'Rock This Town'?

8. For the film *Silence of the Lambs* who won an Oscar for Best Actor, Best Actress and Best Director?

9. In which years were the following people assassinated ?
   A. Malcolm X B. Gianni Versace C. Louis Mountbatten

10. With which songs did the following artists win the Eurovision Song Contest? A. Abba B. Lulu C. Katrina and the Waves

---

ANSWERS

1. Barbara, Janet & Pamela 2. A. *Grange Hill* B. *The Grimleys* C. *The Simpsons* 3. Vince Hill, Benny Hill & Chris Hill 4. Donald Sutherland, James Garner & Tommy Lee Jones 5. A. Charles Kingsley B. Charles Darwin C. Charles Richter 6. Yellow, green & white with red dots 7. A. Curiosity Killed The Cat B. Cat Stevens C. The Stray Cats 8. Anthony Hopkins, Jodie Foster & Johnathan Demme 9. A. 1965 B. 1997 C. 1979 10. A. 'Waterloo' B. 'Boom-Bang-A-Bang' C. 'Love Shine A Light'

QUIZ TWO

1. What are the three official languages of Belgium?
2. In which novels do the following Captains appear? A. Captain Nemo B. Captain Dobbin C. Captain Yossarian
3. Which countries have the three longest coastlines in the world?
4. After Adam & Eve who are the next three people mentioned in the Bible?
5. What would your job be if you were a member of the following Unions? A. NUT B. COHSE C. BALPA
6. What are the first names of the following duos? A. Abbot & Costello B. Hale & Pace C. The Dukes of Hazzard
7. In the year 2000 who were Wimbledon's top three seeded female tennis players?
8. Name the actresses that were killed in the bathroom in the following films. A. *Psycho* B. *Fatal Attraction* C. *Dressed to Kill*
9. Name the three cities all of which begin with the same letter that hosted the Summer Olympics in 1972, 1976 & 1980 respectively.
10. In the human eye what name is given to the A. Coloured part B. Light-sensitive portion C. The white of the eye?

QUIZ THREE

1. Who plays the following lawyers on TV? A. Perry Mason
   B. Petrocelli C. Ally McBeal

2. In 1984 and 1985 name the three artists who had a hit with a
   song called 'The Power of Love'.

3. Name the actors who wore an eye patch in the following films.
   A. *True Grit* B. *Escape From New York* C. *The Vikings*

4. What three words represent the initials QVC in the name of the
   TV shopping channel?

5. What three things beginning with the letter J were the following
   men credited with inventing? A. Levi Strauss B. Frank Whittle
   C. George Spilsbury

6. Name the three songs that topped the UK singles chart
   for 10cc.

7. Who were the last three jockeys to ride over 900 National Hunt
   winners in the 20th century?

8. Who played twins in the following films? A. 1961- *The Parent Trap*
   B. 1988 - *Dead Ringers* C. 1992 - *Raising Cain*

9. Which three European countries lie on the shores of Lake
   Constance?

10. Who played Inspector Clouseau in the following films? A. 1977-
    The Pink Panther Strikes Again B. 1968- *Inspector Clouseau*
    C. 1993– *Son of the Pink Panther*

QUIZ FOUR

1. What are the last three words in the lyrics of the song 'Bohemian Rhapsody'?

2. After New York which three cities in the USA boast the most skyscrapers?

3. What were the 'Brown' hits of the following recording artists? A. Rolling Stones B. Boney M C. The Stranglers

4. Which authors were portrayed in the following films? A. *Time After Time* B. *The Lost Boys* C. *Shadowlands*

5. What are the three longest rivers in the British Isles?

6. Name the three artists who surnames began with O' to have UK No. 1 hits in the 20th century.

7. In which films did the following stars make their big screen debut? A. Orson Welles B. Eddie Murphy C. Whoopi Goldberg

8. Who provided the voice for A. Paddington Bear B. Wallace & Grommit C. Lady Penelope?

9. Which three counties form a border with Norfolk?

10. By what names were the following Wild West heroes better known? A. William Cody B. William Bonney C. Robert Leroy Parker

ANSWERS

1. The wind blows 2. Chicago, Los Angeles & Houston 3. A. 'Brown Sugar' B. 'Brown Girl in the Ring' C. 'Golden Brown' 4. A. HG Wells B. JM Barrie C. CS Lewis 5. Shannon, Severn & Thames 6. Des O'Connor, Sinead O'Connor & Gilbert O'Sullivan 7. A. *Citizen Kane* B. *48 Hours* C. *The Colour Purple* 8. A. Sir Michael Hordern B. Peter Sallis C. Sylvia Anderson 9. Suffolk, Lincolnshire & Cambridgeshire 10. A. Buffalo Bill B. Billy the Kid C. Butch Cassidy

6

QUIZ FIVE

1. Who won Best Actor Oscar for the following films? A. *Scent of a Woman* B. *Leaving Las Vegas* C. *Tender Mercies*

2. Who won Best Actress Oscar for the following films?
   A. *Howard's End* B. *Driving Miss Daisy* C. *A Touch of Class*

3. Who won Best Director Oscar for the following films? A. *Born On The 4th of July* B. *Reds* C. *Amadeus*

4. Name the three films of the 20th century beginning with the letter G that won 8 Oscars or more.

5. Name the three films of the 20th century that earned an Oscar for Jack Nicholson.

6. In which films do the following Oscar-winning songs feature?
   A. 'The Time Of My Life' B. 'Up Where We Belong'
   C. 'Evergreen'

7. Which three films of 1993, 1994 & 1995 earned Tom Hanks an Oscar nomination?

8. Which three films that won the Best Film Oscar in the 1960s were based on true life events?

9. Which films beginning with the letter O won Best Film Oscar in A. 1985 B. 1954 C. 1980?

10. Name the only three films of the 20th century to win 10 Oscars or more.

QUIZ SIX

1. Excluding New Mexico which three American states form a border with Mexico?

2. Starting from the centre what are the first three colours on an archery target?

3. When Kevin Costner played Robin Hood who played A. Friar Tuck B. King Richard C. Will Scarlett?

4. Sandie Shaw was the only female singer to have three No. 1 hit singles in the 1960s. Name the three songs.

5. Who are the three male murder suspects in the board game of Cluedo?

6. Who is the chief God of A. Norse mythology B. Roman mythology C. Egyptian mythology?

7. Name the three songs that topped the singles charts for John Lennon in the two months after his death.

8. Name the three countries, whose names end with the letter A, that form a coastline with the Black Sea.

9. In the nursery rhyme what three things did Old King Cole call for?

10. Who created the following fictional detectives? A. Lord Peter Wimsey B. Cadfael C. Charlie Chan

ANSWERS

1. California, Texas & Arizona 2. Yellow, red & blue 3. A. Mike McShane B. Sean Connery C. Christian Slater 4. 'There's Always Something There To Remind Me', 'Long Live Love' & 'Puppet On A String' 5. Professor Plum, Reverend Green & Colonel Mustard 6. A. Odin B. Jupiter C. Ammon 7. 'Starting Over', 'Woman', & 'Imagine' 8. Russia, Bulgaria & Georgia 9. Pipe, bowl and fiddlers three 10. A. Dorothy Sayers B. Ellis Peters C. Earl Biggers

QUIZ SEVEN

1. Who were the last three wives of Henry VIII?
2. What are the three largest TV companies in the USA?
3. In which years did the following people die? A. Donald Campbell
   B. Peter Cook C. Bill Haley
4. Between 1970 and the year 2000 name the three football clubs
   beginning with the letter W that were promoted to the
   Football League.
5. What are the names of the three universities of the city
   of Birmingham?
6. Name the actor and two actresses who shared a flat in the
   sitcom *Man About the House*.
7. Which were the first three Asian countries to play test cricket?
8. In which towns are the following TV series set? A. *A Touch of
   Frost* B. *Juliet Bravo* C. *The Flying Doctors*
9. Name the 'banana' hits for the following artists. A. The
   Boomtown Rats B. Harry Belafonte C. The Wombles
10. Name the three films of the 1980s that co-starred Michael
    Douglas, Kathleen Turner & Danny DeVito.

QUIZ EIGHT

1. What are the three most popular names for the Pope?

2. Who were the three British Kings of 1936?

3. In the 20th century who were the last three men to feature on the back of a £20 note?

4. Who created the following 'Billy' characters? A. Billy Bunter B. Billy Liar C. Billy Budd

5. Throughout the duration of the TV series *Bilko*, what three ranks were held by Bilko?

6. In which cities were the following people assassinated? A. Archduke Ferdinand B. John F Kennedy C. Leon Trotsky

7. Where in England would you visit A. The National Horse Racing Museum B. The National Railway Museum C. The National Lifeboat Museum?

8. What were the first three years in which Steve Redgrave won an Olympic gold medal?

9. What were the first three league clubs to be managed by Ron Atkinson?

10. Which three American states begin with the letter O?

QUIZ NINE

1. Singapore has four official languages, one of which is Chinese. Name the other three.

2. At the end of the 20th century who were the first three people in line to the British throne?

3. Name the three Wilson brothers who were founder members of the Beach Boys.

4. In greyhound racing what colour jackets are worn by dogs in traps 1, 2 and 3?

5. Name the three consecutive years in which Marc Bolan, Keith Moon and Sid Vicious died.

6. What were the first names of Ken Barlow's first three wives in *Coronation Street*?

7. Name the three hits by Elvis Presley that contain the word 'Heart' in the title of the song.

8. What are the longest rivers in A. France B. Portugal C. Spain?

9. What are the former names of A. Iran B. Sri Lanka C. Ethiopia?

10. What are the three largest islands in the Mediterranean Sea?

ANSWERS

1. English, Malay & Tamil 2. Prince Charles, Prince William & Prince Harry 3. Carl, Dennis & Brian 4. 1 = red, 2 = blue and 3 = white 5. 1977, 1978 & 1979 6. Valerie, Janet and Deirdre 7. 'Heartbreak Hotel', 'Wooden Heart' & 'One Broken Heart For Sale' 8. A. Loire B. Tagus C. Ebro 9. A. Persia B. Ceylon C. Abyssinia 10. Sicily, Sardinia & Cyprus

QUIZ TEN

....

1. Pete, Stuart and Tony were all one-time members of the Beatles. What are their surnames ?

2. Name the three Top 10 hits by Dusty Springfield, the titles of which began with the word 'I'.

3. In 1998 name the three all-girl groups that topped the UK singles charts.

4. What were the first three UK No. 1 hit singles of Abba?

5. Name the three members of the rock trio Cream.

6. Name the three artists who charted with the song 'Some Guys Have All The Luck'.

7. Name the three Top 10 hits for the Beach Boys that contained a first name in the title of the song.

8. Which three groups beginning with the letter K topped the UK singles charts in the 1980s?

9. Who were the three members of the pop group the Police?

10. Name the three pop stars who died in a plane crash in Iowa in 1959.

ANSWERS

1. Best, Sutcliffe & Sheridan 2. 'I Only Want To Be With You,', 'I Just Don't Know What To Do With Myself' & 'I Close My Eyes And Count To Ten' 3. All Saints, Spice Girls & Bewitched 4. 'Waterloo', 'Mamma Mia' & 'Fernando' 5. Eric Clapton, Ginger Baker & Jack Bruce 6. Rod Stewart, Robert Palmer & Maxi Priest 7. 'Barbara Ann','Sloop John B' & 'Lady Lynda' 8. Kraftwerk, Kajagoogoo & KC and the Sunshine Band 9. Sting, Andy Summers & Stuart Copeland 10. Buddy Holly, Richie Valens & the Big Bopper

QUIZ ONE

1. What are the three middle names of Prince Charles?

2. What make of cars are driven by A. Arthur Daley B. Mr Bean
   C. Starsky & Hutch?

3. What are the three largest countries in Africa?

4. What were the first three Carry On films?

5. What are the three main constituents of gunpowder?

6. Following the departure of Peter Gabriel the pop group Genesis
   released an album entitled *And Then There Were Three*. Who were
   the three remaining members?

7. Which three countries were granted membership of NATO on
   14 July 1997?

8. Name the three Brazilian drivers who were Formula One World
   Champions in the 20th century.

9. Which TV programmes were set in the following Scottish towns?
   A. Tannochbrae B. Lochdubh C. Glendarroch

10. Excluding the UK which three countries declared war on
    Germany in 1939?

ANSWERS
1. Phillip Arthur George 2. A. Jaguar B. Mini C. Ford Torino 3. Sudan, Algeria & Zaire
4. *Carry On Sergeant, Carry On Nurse & Carry On Teacher* 5. Charcoal, sulphur & potassium
nitrate 6. Phil Collins, Mike Rutherford & Tony Banks 7. The Czech Republic, Hungary &
Poland. 8. Emerson Fittapaldi, Nelson Piquet & Ayrton Senna 9. A. *Dr Finlay's Casebook*
B. *Hamish Macbeth* C. *Take the High Road* 10. Australia, New Zealand & France

QUIZ TWO

1. Alphabetically what are the first three counties in Northern Ireland?

2. What are the surnames of the three men who shared a 1962 Nobel Prize for their work on DNA research?

3. Name the three British men who won a track 100 metres Olympic gold medal in the 20th century.

4. Which wars were fought between the following years? A. 1839-1842 B. 1775-1783 C. 1899-1902

5. In which novels do the following characters feature?
   A. Man Friday B. Simon Legree C. Oliver Barret IV

6. What are the names of the three main battles fought during the English Civil War?

7. What are the three longest mountain ranges in the world?

8. Name the three World Cup winning footballers who appeared in the film *Escape to Victory*

9. What are the three tallest birds in the world all of which are flightless?

10. In which cities in the UK would you find the following prisons?
    A. Barlinnie B. Winson Green C. Armley

ANSWERS

1. Antrim, Armagh & Derry 2. Crick, Watson & Wilkins 3. Harold Abrahams, Alan Wells & Linford Christie 4. A. The Opium Wars B. The American War of Independence C. The Boer War 5. A. Robinson Crusoe B. Uncle Tom's Cabin C. Love Story 6. Edgehill, Naseby & Marston Moor 7. Andes, Rocky Mountains & Himalayas 8. Bobby Moore, Pele & Ossie Ardiles 9. Ostrich, emu & cassowary 10. A. Glasgow B. Birmingham C. Leeds

QUIZ THREE

1. Excluding Jesus or Christ which three names receive the most mentions in the Bible?

2. Name the three countries beginning with the letter E that form a border with Sudan.

3. Name the Andrew Lloyd Webber musicals that featured the following songs. A. 'Memory' B. 'No Matter What' C. 'I Don't Know How To Love Him'

4. Which film stars won a Best Supporting Actor Oscar for A. *Arthur* B. *Cocoon* C. *A Fish Called Wanda*?

5. Which film stars won a Best Supporting Actress Oscar for? A. *Tootsie* B. *My Left Foot* C. *The Accidental Tourist*?

6. What were the first three capital cities in the world to open an underground railway system?

7. What Apollo numbers made the first three moon landings?

8. Who were the first three Roman Emperors?

9. What are the three secondary colours?

10. Name the three American Presidents of the 1970s.

QUIZ FOUR

1. What are the three most highly populated cities in South America?
2. What is the administrative centre of the following counties?
   A. The Isle of Wight B. Kent C. Shropshire
3. What are the three most common elements in sea water?
4. In the phonetic alphabet what words represent X, Y, Z?
5. Which three countries joined the EU in 1973?
6. Which of the Brontes wrote A. *Agnes Grey* B. *Wuthering Heights*
   C. *Jane Eyre*?
7. Which countries have the following international car registration plates? A. GBZ B. CH C. TT
8. Which three planets of our solar system have the most satellites?
9. Who painted A. *The Birth of Venus* B. *The Laughing Cavalier*
   C. *The Scream*?
10. In which cities were the following orchestras founded A. Halle
    B. The Israel Philharmonic C. The Santa Cecilia Academy?

ANSWERS

1. Sao Paulo, Rio de Janeiro & Buenos Aires 2. A. Newport B. Maidstone C. Shrewsbury
3. Hydrogen, oxygen & chlorine 4. X-ray, Yankee & Zulu 5. UK, Republic of Ireland &
Denmark 6. A. Anne B. Emily C. Charlotte 7. A. Gibraltar B. Switzerland C. Trinidad &
Tobago 8. Saturn, Jupiter & Uranus 9. A. Botticelli B. Franz Hals C. Edvard Munch
10. A. Manchester B. Tel Aviv C. Rome

69

QUIZ FIVE

1. On which islands are the following films set? A. *Shirley Valentine* B. *Papillon* C. *Zorba the Greek*

2. What are the three largest islands in the Indian Ocean?

3. Who had hits with the following songs? A. 'Fantasy Island' B. 'Living On An Island' C. 'Rock Island Line'

4. Who wrote the following novels? A. *Treasure Island* B. *Coral Island* C. *The Island of Dr Moreau*

5. What are the three main Balearic Islands?

6. What is the capital city of A. Cyprus B. The Isle of Man C. The Seychelles?

7. Which countries do the following islands belong to? A. Galapagos B. Azores C. Faroe Islands

8. Who were the first three hosts of *Desert Island Discs*?

9. The following islands belong to which British group of islands? A. St Mary's B. Skye C. Yell

10. The following islands are the largest in which island group? A. Rhodes B. Corfu C. Bougainville

QUIZ SIX

1. What are the three largest states in Australia?
2. In the 1990s which three countries beginning with the letter S won the World Curling Championships for men?
3. In *EastEnders* who played Angie, Den and Sharon Watts?
4. Name the three British monarchs who reigned for less than a year.
5. Name the three counties of the Republic of Ireland that begin with the letter K.
6. Who are the three gods of the Hindu trinity?
7. There are four sections in a symphony orchestra, one of which is the strings. Name the other three.
8. What are the three most highly populated cities in Africa?
9. In *Emmerdale* who plays A. Seth Armstrong B. Alan Turner C. Joe Sugden?
10. What is the state capital of A. Kentucky B. New Mexico C. Hawaii?

ANSWERS

1. Western Australia, Queensland & Northern Territories 2. Scotland, Switzerland & Sweden 3. Anita Dobson, Leslie Grantham and Letitia Dean 4. Edward VIII, Edward V & Lady Jane Grey 5. Kerry, Kildare & Kilkenny 6. Brahma, Vishnu & Shiva 7. Brass, woodwind & percussion 8. Lagos, Cairo & Kinshasa 9. A. Stan Richards B. Richard Thorpe C. Frazier Hines 10. A. Frankfort B. Santa Fe C. Honolulu

QUIZ SEVEN

1. Which of the biblical evangelists are represented by the following symbols? A. An eagle B. A lion C. An ox

2. Name the three American states whose names begin and end with the letter A.

3. Normandy, Plantagenet, Lancaster and York were the first four Royal Houses. What were the next three?

4. By what three ways can heat energy be transferred?

5. What are the three jointed parts of an insect's body called?

6. On what dates of the year are A. Burns Night B. Midsummer Day C. St David's Day?

7. What three countries are collectively known as the Benelux countries?

8. What are the names of the three rabbits that accompany Peter Rabbit in *The Tales of Beatrix Potter*?

9. Which three horse races make up the American Triple Crown?

10. What three words are the names given to the three Christian monastic vows?

QUIZ EIGHT

1. What are the three most highly populated cities in Europe?

2. The Battle of Balaklava gave its name to which three new English words, all relating to clothing?

3. What are the three highest ranks of angel?

4. Name the three reindeers of Santa whose names begin with the letter D.

5. Which of the seven ancient wonders of the world could be found at A. Babylon B. Olympia C. Rhodes?

6. Which three species of Rhino are named after their places of origin?

7. What are the three main colours of seaweed?

8. Which three powers fought with Great Britain against Russia in the Crimean War?

9. What are the first three films featuring the characters of Wallace & Grommit?

10. In the TV series *Black Adder* who played? A. Richard III B. Elizabeth I C. Richard IV

ANSWERS

1. Moscow, London & Paris 2. Balaclava, cardigan & raglan 3. Seraphim, cherubim & thrones 4. Dancer, Dasher & Donner 5. A. Hanging gardens B. Statue of Zeus C. The Colossus 6. Indian, Javan & Sumatran 7. Red, green & brown 8. France, Turkey & Sardinia 9. *A Grand Day Out, The Wrong Trousers* & *A Close Shave* 10. A. Peter Cook B. Miranda Richardson C. Brian Blessed

QUIZ NINE

1. What are the first names of the Oscar-winning film stars, from the three generations of the Huston family?

2. What three things did God create on the fourth day?

3. What are the three highest mountains in Europe?

4. What three things grow in the garden of Mary, Mary quite contrary?

5. The crosses of which three Saints appear on the Union flag?

6. Which 'quintets' had hits with A. 'Doctor My Eyes' B. 'Glad All Over' C. 'Mockingbird Hill'

7. What are the names of the three fairy godmothers in *Sleeping Beauty*?

8. What name is given to the young of a A. Cranefly B. Squirrel C. Pike?

9. Who were the three reigning English monarchs of the 17th century?

10. In the film *The Krays* who played the twins and their mother?

QUIZ TEN

1. According to the Bible, God sent gnats and which other three creatures to plague the Egyptians?

2. What are the names of Donald Duck's nephews?

3. What three species of snake are native to Great Britain?

4. What is the collective name for a group of A. Lions B. Leopards C. Rhinos?

5. In which three years did Red Rum win the Grand National?

6. What is the collective name for a group of A. Swans B. Peacocks C. Parrots?

7. What is the name of the lion in A. *The Lion King* B. *The Lion, The Witch And The Wardrobe* C. *Daktari*?

8. What is the name of the dog in A. *The Famous Five* B. *The Secret Seven* C. *Little Orphan Annie*?

9. Where do the following bears live? A. Yogi Bear B. Rupert the Bear C. Winnie the Pooh

10. Excluding sheep which three animals can be classed as angora?

QUIZ ONE

1. What are the currencies, all beginning with the letter R, of the following countries? A. South Africa B. Saudi Arabia C. Indonesia

2. In which novels do the following characters appear? A. Tom Canty B. John Jarndyce C. John Blackthorne

3. What are the literal English translations of the following foreign phrases? A. Déjà vu B. In camera C. Compos mentis

4. Who released the following pop albums? A. *Can't Slow Down* B. *No Parlez* C. *Ten Good Reasons*

5. Name the car manufacturers that make the following models. A. Uno B. Corolla C. Quattro

6. The Eurovision Song Contest of 1969 ended in a four-way tie. Which three nations tied with the UK?

7. Name the TV sitcoms that are set at A. The Whitbury Leisure Centre B. Oil Drum Lane C. The Bayview Retirement Home

8. Name the lead singers of A. The Bay City Rollers B. Spandau Ballet C. Guns 'n' Roses

9. What were the first names of E Nesbit's Railway Children?

10. In the 1970 film of *The Railway Children* who played the children?

ANSWERS

1. A. Rand B. Riyal C. Rupiah 2. A. *The Prince and the Pauper* B. *Bleak House* C. *Shogun* 3. A. Already seen B. In secret C. In right mind 4. A. Lionel Richie B. Paul Young C. Jason Donovan 5. A. Fiat B. Toyota C. Audi 6. A. France, Spain & Holland 7. A. *The Brittas Empire* B. *Steptoe & Son* C. *Waiting For God* 8. A. Les McKeown B. Tony Hadley C. Axl Rose 9. Roberta, Peter and Phyllis 10. Jenny Agutter, Gary Warren and Sally Thomsett

QUIZ TWO

1. Name Britain's three Prime Ministers of the 1930s.

2. Lake Victoria is bounded by which three countries?

3. What are the state capitals of A. New South Wales B. Tasmania C. Victoria?

4. In the drama series *The Boys From The Blackstuff* who played A. Chrissy B. The wife of Chrissy C. Yosser Hughes?

5. Name the three capitals of South Africa each used for a different function.

6. Name the three films all containing the word 'man' that starred Dustin Hoffman in the following years A. 1988 B. 1976 C. 1970.

7. What are the names of the three groups into which diamonds are categorized?

8. What are the three most highly populated cities in Asia?

9. What are the names of the pubs in A. *EastEnders* B. *Emmerdale* C. *Only Fools and Horses*?

10. What are the only three animals that possess ivory tusks?

QUIZ THREE

1. In the sitcom *Yes Prime Minister* who played A. Sir Humphrey Appleby B. Jim Hacker C. Bernard Wooley?

2. Which famous personality was at one time the Mayor of A. Cincinatti B. Carmel C. Palm Springs?

3. What were the 'Baby' No. I hits for A. The Supremes B. The Foundations C. Britney Spears?

4. After World War I the Prime Minister of Britain, the President of the USA and the President of France drew up the Treaty of Versailles. Name those three leaders.

5. In the Royle Family who plays Denise, Jim and Barbara?

6. What are the names of the hospitals that feature in the following TV dramas? A. *St Elsewhere* B. *Angels* C. *Doctor In The House*

7. Who topped the charts with A. 'Maggie May' B. 'January' C. 'December 63'?

8. Name the footballers who married A. Posh Spice B. Louise Durning C. Leslie Ash?

9. Who were the first three male singers with the surname of Jones to have a Top 10 hit single in the UK?

10. The Teenage Mutant Ninja Turtles were all named after famous painters, one of which was Michelangelo. Name the other three.

QUIZ FOUR

1. Who played Fletcher Christian in the following versions of
   Mutiny On The Bounty? A. 1935 - *Mutiny On The Bounty*
   B. 1984 - *The Bounty* C. 1962 - *The Mutiny On The Bounty*

2. Who are the female lead singers of? A. Blondie B. Altered
   Images C. Texas

3. In *Star Trek* who played A. Captain Kirk B. Dr McCoy
   C. Mr Chekov?

4. What are the occupational nicknames of the following football
   teams? A. Walsall B. Luton C. Rotherham

5. There are six official languages in which the United Nations
   conducts business. English, French and Russian are three of
   them, name the other three.

6. Name the 'Blue' groups that had hits with the following songs.
   A. 'Melting Pot' B. 'Hippy, Hippy, Shake' C. 'Breakfast At Tiffany's'

7. What are the three oldest universities in England?

8. In which wars were the following films set? A. *Platoon* B. *MASH*
   C. *The Blue Max*

9. Name the three cities that hosted more than one Summer
   Olympics in the 20th century.

10. Who were the first three Pauls to have a solo No. 1 hit in
    the UK?

QUIZ FIVE

1. In which countries are the following musicals set? A. *Evita*
   B. *Fiddler On The Roof* C. *The King And I.*

2. In which musicals do the following songs appear? A. 'Don't Rain
   On My Parade' B. 'Bless Your Beautiful Hide' C. 'Send In
   The Clowns'

3. Who collaborated with Andrew Lloyd Webber on A. *Cats*
   B. *Starlight Express* C. *The Beautiful Game?*

4. The musical *The Sound Of Music* was A. Based on whose novel
   B. Directed by who C. Set in which city?

5. Who played the title roles in the following film musicals?
   A. 1974- *Mame* B. 1980- *The Jazz Singer* C. 1958- *Gigi*

6. In the film *Grease* A. Who sang 'Beauty School Drop Out'?
   B. Which song opened the film? C. Which school did the
   cast attend?

7. In which stage musicals do the following songs feature?
   A. 'I Know Him So Well' B. 'Good Morning Starshine' C. 'Music
   Of The Night'

8. Which Disney cartoons feature the following songs? A. 'I Wanna
   Be like You' B. 'Under The Sea' C. 'A Whole New World'

9. Name the songs that won a Best Song Oscar from the following
   films. A. *Titanic* B. *White Nights* C. *Top Gun*

10. Which composer's life stories were told in the following films?
    A. *Song of Norway* B. *Song Without End* C. *A Song To Remember*

ANSWERS

1. A. Argentina B. Russia C. Siam 2. A. *Funny Girl* B. *Seven Brides For Seven Brothers*
C. *A Little Night Music* 3. A. Tim Rice B. Richard Stilgoe C. Ben Elton 4. A. Maria Von
Trapp B. Robert Wise C. Salzburg 5. A. Lucille Ball B. Neil Diamond C. Leslie Caron
6. A. Frankie Avalon B. 'Summer Nights' C. Rydell High 7. A. *Chess* B. *Hair* C. *Phantom
Of The Opera* 8. A. *Jungle Book* B. *The Little Mermaid* C. *Aladdin* 9. A. 'My Heart Will Go
On' B. 'Say You, Say Me' C. 'Take My Breath Away' 10. A. Greig B. Liszt C. Chopin

QUIZ SIX

1. In which area of London are the following TV programmes set?
   A. *Only Fools & Horses* B. *Citizen Smith* C. *The Goodies*

2. Which three London football clubs did Terry Venables play for?

3. What three married surnames has Deirdre had in
   Coronation Street?

4. In the Magpie rhyme, one is for sorrow, two for joy, three for a
   girl and four for a boy. What are five, six and seven?

5. Name the two Richards and a Roger that appeared in the film
   The Wild Geese.

6. Over what distances are the following races run? A. The Epsom
   Derby B. The St Leger C. The Greyhound Grand National

7. Name the three English counties that begin with the letter B.

8. What were the names of the wives of the following
   American Presidents? A. Gerald Ford B. Ronald Reagan
   C. Abraham Lincoln

9. Name the three Elvis Presley hits that contain the word 'Blue' in
   the title.

10. What is the name of the butler in the following? A. *Batman*
    B. *Soap* C. *To The Manor Born*

8

QUIZ SEVEN

1. In which American states would you find? A. Orlando
   B. Detroit C. Sacramento

2. Over which three months did the Battle of Britain take place?

3. Name the three 1963 No. I hits for Gerry & the Pacemakers.

4. What are the first names of the following classical composers?
   A. Wagner B. Beethoven C. Verdi

5. On which three oceans does Canada have a coastline?

6. What is removed in the following operations? A. Mastectomy
   B. Gastrectomy C. Orchidectomy

7. Excluding London which three cities in the UK have an Assay
   Office for hallmarking precious metals?

8. What is the home planet of A. Mr Spock B. Luke Skywalker
   C. Dr Who?

9. What are the names of the twins in A. *The Adventures of Tintin* B.
   Hi-De-Hi C. *Alice in Wonderland*?

10. In which American states are the following TV programmes set?
    A. *King of the Hill* B. *Roseanne* C. *South Park*

QUIZ EIGHT

1. What are the three types of nuclear radiation?

2. What are the three colours of the compartments of a roulette wheel?

3. In the film *Four Weddings and a Funeral* who played A. Charles B. Carrie C. The Vicar?

4. Which South American countries form a border with Paraguay?

5. The names of which three animals are terms used to describe types of market on the Stock Exchange?

6. In *EastEnders* what are the first names of the three children of Pauline Fowler?

7. On which rivers do the following cities stand? A. Paris B. Antwerp C. Cologne

8. What are the surnames of A. Ginger Spice B. Baby Spice C. Sporty Spice?

9. What are the names given to the three terms at Oxford University?

10. What were the names of the three Gorgons of Greek mythology?

QUIZ NINE

1. Who were the three husbands of Ava Gardner?

2. Which motorcycle manufacturers made the following models?
   A. Commando B. Bantam C. Electra Glide

3. What are the first names of Stock, Aitken & Waterman?

4. In the sitcom *Cheers*, name the actresses who played A. Diane
   B. Rebecca C. Carla.

5. What three diseases are treated by the MMR vaccine?

6. Name the men who were nicknamed A. The King of Hollywood
   B. The King of Swing C. The March King?

7. What are the names of the three National Parks in Wales?

8. Who wrote the following 'Worldly' novels? A. *Around The World
   In Eighty Days* B. *War of the Worlds* C. *Brave New World*

9. The capitals of the following countries all begin with the letter K.
   Name them. A. Afghanistan B. Ukraine C. Sudan

10. Which three public holidays were introduced into the UK by the
    Bank Holiday Act passed in 1871?

QUIZ TEN

1. In the 1970s there were four flat jockey champions in the UK, one of whom was Lester Piggott. Name the other three.

2. Over what three distances are races run in a heptathlon?

3. When Manchester United beat Benfica in the 1968 European Cup Final, which three players got their names on the score sheet?

4. What names are given to the start of a game in A. Hockey B. Basketball C. Ice Hockey?

5. Name the three British golfers who won the World Matchplay Championships in the 1990s.

6. Name the three swimmers who won Olympic golds for the UK in. A. 1976 B. 1980 C. 1988.

7. In the world of sport what three words are represented by the initials WWF?

8. In the 1990s what were the three venues of the Winter Olympics?

9. Name the three Newcastle United managers of the 1990s who as players won the European Cup.

10. What are the three disciplines of a triathlon?

ANSWERS

1. Pat Eddery, Willie Carson & Joe Mercer 2. 100 metres, 200 metres & 800 metres 3. Bobby Charlton, George Best & Brian Kidd 4. A. Bully off B. Tip off C. Face off 5. Nick Faldo, Ian Woosnam & Colin Montgomerie 6. A. David Wilkie B. Duncan Goodhew C. Adrian Moorhouse 7. World Wrestling Federation 8. 1992 - Albertville 1994 - Lillehammer & 1998 - Nagano 9. Kevin Keegan, Kenny Dalglish & Ruud Gullit 10. Cycling, running & swimming

SESSION 9

QUIZ ONE

1. Who played the father in the following sitcoms? A. *Butterflies*
   B. *Bless This House* C. *Father Dear Father*
2. What are the three most abundant gases in the Earth's atmosphere?
3. Who were the three members of the Supremes when they had their first hit?
4. Name the three cathedral cities that play host to the 'Three Choirs Concerts'.
5. Jamaica is divided into three counties which have the same names as English counties. Name them.
6. Name the three English football league teams whose names are suffixed with the word 'Wanderers'.
7. In which month do the following days fall? A. Bastille Day
   B. Groundhog Day C. Lady Day
8. In *The Muppet Show* what is the name of A. Kermit's nephew
   B. The scientist C. The comic bear?
9. Name the Three Musketeers.
10. What are the three main constituents of gunmetal?

QUIZ TWO

1. Which sitcoms featured the following armed forces characters?
   A. Private Popplewell B. Captain Ashwood C. Colonel Hall

2. What is the name of the following soups? A. Russian beetroot
   soup B. Indian curry soup C. Cold Spanish soup

3. Which three star signs encompass the months of April and May?

4. Which Shakespeare plays feature the following characters?
   A. Robin Goodfellow B. Shylock C. Desdemona

5. By what three names has the largest city in Turkey been known?

6. In which sports are the following trophies contested? A. Uber
   Cup B. Dunhill Cup C. Swaythling Cup

7. In the sitcom *Allo, Allo* who played Edith, Rene and Yvette?

8. Which James Bond theme was sung by A. Tom Jones
   B. Lulu C. Gladys Knight?

9. What is the name of the official residence of A. The President of
   the USA B. The Archbishop of Canterbury C. The Lord Mayor
   of London?

10. Name the three actors who played the title roles in the sitcom
    Filthy, Rich and Catflap.

ANSWERS

1. A. *The Army Game* B. *It Ain't Half Hot Mum* C. Sergeant Bilko 2. A. Borscht B. Mulligatawny C. Gazpacho 3. Aries, Taurus & Gemini 4. A. *A Midsummer's Night's Dream* B. *The Merchant of Venice* C. *Othello* 5. Istanbul, Constantinople & Byzantium 6. A. Badminton B. Golf C. Table Tennis 7. Carmen Silvera, Gordon Kaye and Vicki Michelle 8. A. *Thunderball* B. *The Man With The Golden Gun* C. *Licence To Kill* 9. A. The White House B. Lambeth Palace C. Mansion House 10. Nigel Planer, Rik Mayall and Ade Edmonson

QUIZ THREE

1. What names did Bob Geldof and Paula Yates give to their three children?

2. On which rivers would you find the following dams? A. Aswan B. Kariba C. Hoover

3. What is given as a booby prize in the following game shows? A. *Blankety Blank* B. *3-2-1* C. *Double or Drop*

4. What are the three highest ranks of British nobility?

5. What name is given to the male, female and young of a rabbit?

6. What are the titles of the first three sequels to the 1968 film *Planet of the Apes*?

7. What is the more common name for A. Solid carbon dioxide B. Nitrous oxide C. Iron oxide?

8. Name the three snooker players that Steve Davies beat in the final, to win his first three world titles.

9. What are the middle names, all of which begin with the letter A, of the following people? A. Thomas Edison B. Elvis Presley C. Glen Miller

10. In mainland Europe which country contains A. The most northerly point B. The most southerly point C. The most westerly point?

QUIZ FOUR

1. How many sides do the following have? A. Tetrahedon
   B. Heptagon C. Dodecagon

2. Name the artists who had a Christmas No. 1 with A. 'When A
   Child Is Born' B. 'Only You' C. 'Save Your Love'?

3. What breed of bird are the following? A. Greylag B. Rhode
   Island Red C. Beltsville

4. Which 'black' named groups had hits with? A. 'Agadoo' B. 'Ride
   On Time' C. 'Paranoid'

5. Name the musicals based on the following novels. A. *Goodbye To
   Berlin* B. *Kipp* C. *The Matchmakers*

6. In which decade were the following introduced into the UK?
   A. Zebra crossings B. Driving tests C. Breathalysers

7. Name the *Carry On* films that the following actors appeared in.
   A. Phil Silvers B. Patrick Moore C. Harry H Corbett

8. Name the three players that scored for Manchester United in
   the 1968 European Cup Final.

9. Which rivers did the following artists sing about? A. Enya
   B. Gerry and the Pacemakers C. Lindisfarne

10. Which three English counties have the longest coastline?

ANSWERS
1. A. 4 B. 7 C. 12 2. A. Johnny Mathis B. Flying Pickets C. Renee & Renato 3. A. Goose
B. Chicken C. Turkey 4. A. Black Lace B. Black Box C. Black Sabbath 5. A. *Cabaret*
B. *Half A Sixpence* C. *Hello Dolly* 6. A. 1950s B. 1930s C. 1960s 7. A. *Carry On Follow That
Camel* B. *Carry On England* C. *Carry On Screaming* 8. Bobby Charlton, George Best &
Brian Kidd 9. A. Orinoco B. Mersey C. Tyne 10. Cornwall, Devon & Essex

QUIZ FIVE

1. What are the names of the girlfriends of A. Mickey Mouse B. Donald Duck C. Yogi Bear?

2. Which characters drive the following cars in *Wacky Races*? A. Turbo Terrific B. The Army Surplus Special C. The Convert-A-Car

3. What is the name of Popeye's A. Arch enemy B. Dog C. Father?

4. Top Cat, Choo Choo and Fancy. Which three members of the gang are missing?

5. What are the names of Homer and Marge Simpson's three children?

6. What sort of creatures are the following cartoon characters? A. Foghorn Leghorn B. Pepe Le Pew C. Chilly Willy

7. What are the names of the three human companions of Scooby Doo and Shaggy?

8. Who first voiced the following cartoon characters? A. Bugs Bunny B. Donald Duck C. Dangermouse

9. In Walt Disney films what sort of creatures were the following? A. Monstro in *Pinocchio* B. Shere Khan in *Jungle Book* C. Timothy in *Dumbo*

10. Which cartoon characters had the following catchphrases? A. Heavens to Murgatroyd B. Drat and double drat C. I hate those meeces to pieces

ANSWERS

1. A. Minnie B. Daisy C. Cindy 2. A. Peter Perfect B. Sarge & Meekley C. Professor Pat Pending 3. A. Bluto B. Jeep C. Poopdeck Pappy 4. Brains, Benny the Ball & Spook 5. Bart, Lisa & Maggie 6. A. Rooster B. Skunk C. Penguin 7. Fred, Daphne & Velma 8. A. Mel Blanc B. Clarence Nash C. David Jason 9. A. Whale B. Tiger C. Mouse 10. A. Snagglepuss B. Dick Dastardly C. Mr Jinx

QUIZ SIX

1. Who were the first three post World War II British Prime Ministers?

2. What are the three most frequently used letters in the English language?

3. What are the three titles of Ian Dury's only top 10 hits?

4. In *Dad's Army* who played A. Private Walker B. The ARP Warden C. The Vicar?

5. Which American cities were originally called A. New Amsterdam B. Fort Washington C. Fort Dearborn?

6. Which flower, vegetable and mythical beast are all national symbols for Wales?

7. Which wars were fought between the following years? A. 1338–1453 B. 1455–1485 C. 264 BC–261 BC

8. In which countries are the world's three highest waterfalls?

9. For which TV programmes were the following songs the theme? A. 'Suicide Is Painless' B. 'I Could Be So Good For You' C. 'That's Living All'

10. Through which three European countries does the river Meuse flow?

QUIZ SEVEN

1. What are the stage names of the following entertainers who were born A. Priscilla White B. David White C. William White?

2. In which cities are the following airports? A. Logan airport B. Schiphol airport C. Fiumicino airport

3. What sort of nuts are used in the preparation of A. Marzipan B. Pesto C. Satay sauce?

4. What is the name of the horse of A. Roy Rogers B. Tonto C. Don Quixote?

5. Who played the title roles in the following TV dramas? A. *Jonathan Creek* B. *McCloud* C. *Cadfael*

6. In which decade did the following models of car first appear? A. Ford Escort B. Volkswagen Beetle C. Honda Civic

7. Who were the three English monarchs of 1553?

8. What are the titles of Sheena Easton's three UK top 10 hits of the 20th century?

9. What were the names of the yachts of A. Simon Le Bon B. Edward Heath C. Lady Penelope in *Thunderbirds*?

10. Who won the FA Cup in 1998, 1999 & 2000?

QUIZ EIGHT

1. Which three countries produce the most cars annually?

2. What are Princess Anne's other three first names?

3. In which Dickens novels did the following characters appear?
   A. Little Nell B. Tiny Tim C. Little Emily

4. Who along with Davy Jones made up the Monkees pop group?

5. What colour of shirts are worn by the following Rugby Union nations? A. France B. New Zealand C. Wales

6. In the sitcom *Some Mothers Do 'Ave 'Em* what are the first names of Mr & Mrs Spencer and their daughter?

7. Who had hits with the following 'sexy' songs? A. I Want Your Sex B. Sexual Healing C. Let's Talk About Sex

8. In the classic *Monty Python* Parrot Sketch, who played the shopkeeper and the customer and what breed was the parrot?

9. Who played the leading lady in the 1937, 1954 & 1976 film versions of *A Star Is Born*?

10. Through which three countries does the river Rhine flow?

ANSWERS

1. USA, Japan & Germany 2. Elizabeth, Alice & Louise 3. A. *The Old Curiosity Shop*
B. *A Christmas Carol* C. *David Copperfield* 4. Mike Nesmith, Micky Dolenz & Peter Tork
5. A. Blue B. Black C. Red 6. Frank, Betty & Jessica 7. A. George Michael B. Marvin
Gaye C. Salt 'n' Pepa 8. Michael Palin, John Cleese and a Norwegian Blue 9. 1937 - Janet
Gaynor, 1954 - Judy Garland & 1976 - Barbara Streisand 10. Holland, Germany
& Switzerland

QUIZ NINE

1. What is the name of the fairy, the dog and the ship in Peter Pan?

2. What is added to A. Curry to make it yellow B. Pasta to make it green C. Gin to make it pink?

3. What are the three largest National Parks in England?

4. The following phobias are the morbid fear of what?
   A. Acrophobia B. Necrophobia C. Emetophobia

5. Who created the following children's book characters? A. Willy Wonka B. Thomas the Tank Engine C. Noddy

6. Who sang the following songs about Liverpool? A. 'Long Haired Lover From Liverpool' B. 'Liverpool Lou' C. 'Going Down To Liverpool'

7. What are the names of the Parliaments of A. USA B. Japan C. Spain?

8. In the song 'The Twelve Days Of Christmas' what gifts were given on the first three days?

9. Who had hits with A. 'Cathy's Clown' B. 'Tears of a Clown' C. 'Ha Ha Said The Clown'?

10. What name is given to the home of a A. Beaver B. Otter C. Wolf?

QUIZ TEN

1. What are the only three Brazilian cities that are home to a British Embassy or Consulate?

2. Name the three English cities beginning with the letter N.

3. Name the three American states beginning with the letter O.

4. What are the names of the three piers in the resort of Blackpool?

5. Excluding Egypt, through which three countries does the river Nile flow?

6. What are the three largest cities standing on the river Danube?

7. There are four time-zones in the USA, one of which is Eastern. Name the other three.

8. What are the names of the national airlines of A. Australia B. Brazil C. Hungary?

9. What are the state capitals of the following, all of which have a French-sounding name? A. Iowa B. South Dakota C. Louisiana

10. What were the first three bridges to built across the river Thames?

ANSWERS

1. Rio de Janeiro, Brasilia & Sao Paulo 2. Newcastle Upon Tyne, Norwich & Nottingham 3. Ohio, Oklahoma & Oregon 4. North, South and Central 5. Tanzania, Sudan & Uganda 6. Vienna, Budapest & Belgrade 7. Central, Mountain and Pacific 8. A. Qantas B. Varig C. Malev 9. A. Des Moines B. Pierre C. Baton Rouge 10. London Bridge, Kingston Bridge & Putney Bridge